Year 9
ALGEBRA
CORE

Unit		Page
1	Numbers and calculators	2
2	Shapes and numbers	8
3	Sequences and mappings	17
4	Numbers from patterns	28
5	Exploring numbers	36
6	Moving shapes	44
7	Exploring graphs	49
8	Spreadsheets and sequences	54
9	Making and solving equations	59

Symbols in the margin

- ✓ Special things you *will* need
- ○ Special things you *may* need
- Worksheet reference (G refers to graphic calculator worksheet)
- Work for a graphic calculator here
- Work for a computer here (screen may show one of these **D** Database **G** Graph plotter **S** Spreadsheet **L** Logo)

LD Logo 2000 disk
LN Logo 2000 documentation
LP LogoPack

Unit 1 Numbers and calculators

Fair shares

1. If £4 is shared between five people, how much does each person have?

2. If £8 is shared between ten people, how much does each have?

3. Why are your answers the same for questions 1 and 2?

4. If you share 60 conkers between 12 children, how many does each child have?

5. If you share 20 conkers between four children, how many does each have?

6. Why are your answers the same?

■ Use these two diagrams to make up a pair of questions that give the same answer.

■ On your calculator, do two shared by seven – **2** **÷** **7**

7. Write down your answer.

8. Can you find another pair of numbers that gives the same answer?

2 **÷** **7** *can be written $\frac{2}{7}$*

On a computer keyboard you will not find a **÷** *key.*

Instead there is a **/** *key.*

■ In Logo, type:

PR 2/7

or check some of the earlier questions on sharing.

LP A1

... Numbers and calculators

Calculator pairs

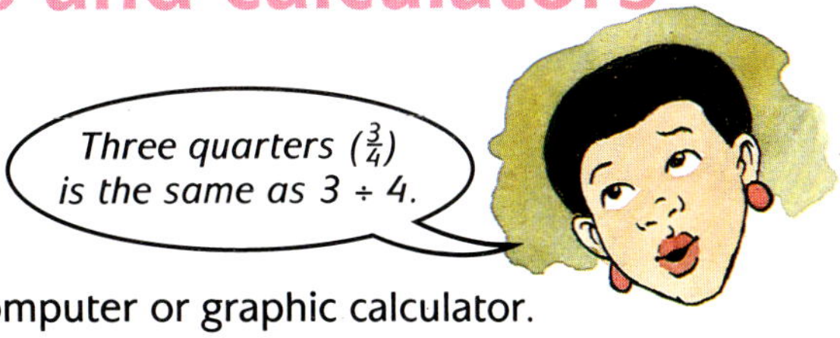

Three quarters ($\frac{3}{4}$) is the same as 3 ÷ 4.

Use a calculator, computer or graphic calculator.

■ Check that $\frac{3}{4}$ = 0.75.

■ Find as many pairs of numbers as you can that give 0.75.
(There are seven pairs where both numbers are less than 30.)

1. Find the missing number;

    30/? = 0.75

    ?/60 = 0.75

    75/? = 0.75

    5/6 = 0.83333 . . .

■ Find six pairs of numbers that give the same answer.

□ Explain in writing any quick way you discovered for finding the number pairs.

Matching fractions

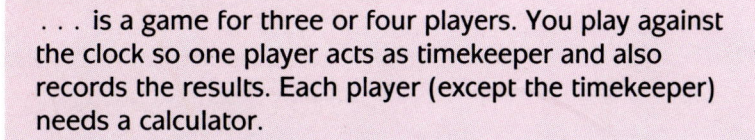

. . . is a game for three or four players. You play against the clock so one player acts as timekeeper and also records the results. Each player (except the timekeeper) needs a calculator.

Choose two numbers and divide them. See how many pairs of numbers you can find in 60 seconds.

Choose a new pair of numbers to start and try to beat your record.

2. Find the missing numbers:

    4/7 = 12/?

    2/9 = ?/36

    20/? = 100/85

    ?/45 = 7/9

■ Make up three of your own.

Y 9 ALGEBRA – C

... Numbers and calculators

Turning the tables

*What are **multiples**?*

5, 10, 15, 20 and 25 are the first five multiples of 5.

1. Write out the first ten **multiples** of nine.
2. Write down any patterns you find.
3. Does the pattern continue when you keep going?
4. What happens when you add the digits (the single bits that make up the number)?

   eg. 18 → 1 + 8 → 9

It is easy to find multiples of nine.

5. Which of these numbers divides exactly by nine:

   207, 315, 721, 783, 2106, 5563?

- Use a calculator to check.
- Write down a rule that will help you to find numbers that divide exactly by nine.

The numbers below all divide exactly by nine but some digits have been smudged.

6. Can you find the missing digits?

   22■1, ■62, 56■3, 693■, 450■8

The idea of adding digits is helpful when you look at multiples of three.

- Write down some multiples of three.
- Can you find a rule to help you find multiples of three?

- Write down some multiples of five.
- What can you say about all multiples of five?

- Combine your rules to write down some multiples of 15.
- Check your prediction with a calculator.

7. Which of these numbers is a multiple of 15:

   270, 1005, 7062, 545, 495?

- Can you make a rule for multiples of six?
- Check your prediction.

... Numbers and calculators

Grass cutting

A school pays three people £80 each to cut the school playing-fields. Later in the term, the school pays a team of six people £40 each to do the same job.

1. How much did the school pay out on each occasion?

■ Explain your answer to a friend.

■ Find some more pairs of numbers that give the same result.

2. Find the missing number:

   5 × 8 = 10 × ?

   5 × 12 = 10 × ?

   5 × 22 = 10 × ?

   5 × 68 = 10 × ?

■ What happens when the number is odd?

3. Work out 5 × 47.

■ Make up three of your own.

Double trouble

Sometimes a quick way of multiplying by four is to double and double again:

   23 × 4   double 23 is 46   double 46 is 92

4. Do these in your head as quickly as you can:

   32 × 4, 122 × 4, 4 × 35, 4 × 307, 99 × 4.

■ Work with a partner. Use a calculator. See if you can do some calculations like these faster than your partner.

Double 32 is . . .

Y 9 ALGEBRA – C

... Numbers and calculators

Frogs

✓ up to 12 counters of two different colours or pegboard and pegs

On a row of five squares, two red counters and two white counters are placed like this.

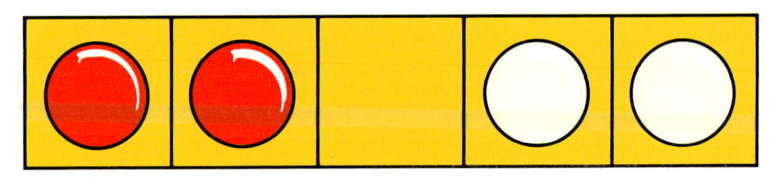

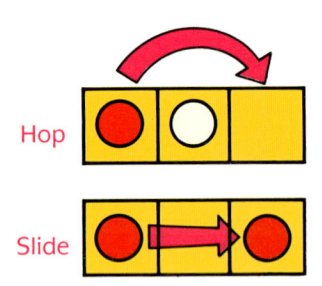

Hop

Slide

Red counters move to the left; white counters move to the right.

Can you finish with the white counters where the red ones are and the red counters where the white ones are?

☐ When you have solved this puzzle, write down how you did it.

Ask your partner to follow your instructions.

■ Try to explain the moves in a clearer or shorter way.

[1] How many moves does it take?

■ Can you do it in fewer moves? Try!

☐ Try it with a different number of counters, for example three of each colour.

■ Repeat the problem with different numbers of counters.

☐ Record how many moves you take each time.

Check your answers with your partner; it is easy to make a mistake.

■ Look for patterns in your results.

■ How many moves would it take if you had the whole class in two teams?

Persuade your teacher to let you check your prediction!

... Numbers and calculators

One, two, three, four

What are the brackets there for?

We must do what's in the brackets first.

■ Use the digits 1, 2, 3 and 4 like this:

$1 \times (2 + 3) - 4 = 1$

$(3 + 1) \div (4 - 2) = 2$

$1 \times 2 \times 3 \times 4 = 24$

We can use the operations $+$, $-$, $\times$ and $\div$.

■ How many different statements can you find?

1. Is 24 the highest number you can make?
2. How many of the numbers from one to twenty four can you make in this way?
   - Write down all your answers.
   - How could you extend the problem?

Five under ten

This is a game for two or more players.

One person writes down five numbers under ten.

$$1 \quad 3 \quad 7 \quad 5 \quad 6$$

Another person writes down a number between 100 and 200.

This is the target. 117

Players have to use all the five numbers to make another number.

The nearest to the target number wins a point.

$$3(6 \times 7) - 5 - 1 = 120$$

$$3(5 \times 7) + 6 + 1 = 112$$

- Keep score.
- Choose new numbers.
- The first person to ten wins.

Y 9 ALGEBRA – C

Unit 2 Shapes and numbers

Building with numbers

25 – square

1	2	3	~~4~~	5
~~6~~	7	~~8~~	9	10
11	12	13	14	15
16	17	18	19	20
21	22	23	24	25

1. Using only **2** and **×** what numbers can you make which total less than 25?

   2 × 2 × 2 is 8

2. Using **2** **3** and **×** make some more numbers less than 25.
3. Try using **2** **3** **5** and **×** to make numbers less than 25.
4. Repeat question 3 with **2** **3** **5** **7** and **×**.
5. Why is there no point in using four or six to make new numbers with?

   *Numbers like two, three, five and seven are called **prime** numbers.*

   Numbers like four, six and eight are not prime numbers because they can be built from other numbers:

   $$4 = 2 × 2$$
   $$6 = 2 × 3$$
   $$8 = 2 × 2 × 2$$

6. What is the next prime number after seven?

   ■ Use it to build some more numbers less than 25.

   ☐ Take a 25-square and cross out all the numbers you have made so far.

   ☐ Make a list of all the numbers you have left.

   These are prime numbers.

   ☐ Check your list to make sure that none of the primes can be built by multiplying together a pair of smaller numbers.

   Beware! *1 is not a prime number. You cannot build with it:*

   $$1 × 1 × 1 × 1 \ldots = ?$$

... Shapes and numbers

Testing for primes

*Is 105 a **prime number**?*

*105 ends in five... so it must have been made using five. Five is a **factor**.*

Yes and 105 ÷ 5 = 21

Twenty-one is not a prime because 21 = 3 × 7

■ So 105 is built from five, three and seven.

Five, three and seven are **factors** of 105.

☐ How do you know that three is a factor of 105? (See 'Turning the tables' on page 4.)

☐ Test the numbers between 100 and 120 to see which ones are prime and which have been built from other numbers.

101	102	103	104	105
106	107	108	109	110
111	112	113	114	115
116	117	118	119	120

Y 9 ALGEBRA – C

... Shapes and numbers

**Pictures for numbers
... the number line**

Use the number line worksheet.

Starting at zero, move in steps of two:

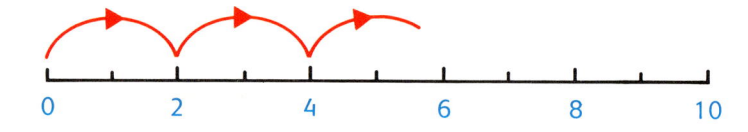

0   2   4   6   8   10

[1] What numbers do you get?

[2] Write down the first ten numbers you arrive at.

This time start at one.

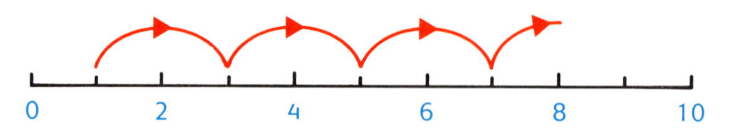

0   2   4   6   8   10

[3] What numbers do you get now?

[4] Try using steps of three instead of two.

■ Try taking bigger steps each jump.

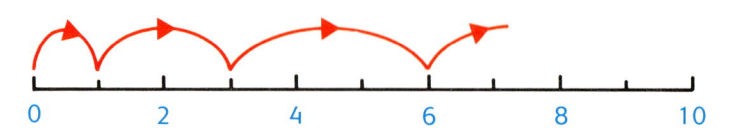

0   2   4   6   8   10

[5] What pattern do these steps give?

■ Make up three of your own.

I'm going to start at one and move in steps of five.

What would happen if you started that at zero?

... Shapes and numbers

... rectangle numbers

✓ counters or pegs and pegboard

Take a set of counters (not more than 25) and arrange them in a rectangle:

Here are 15 counters placed in a rectangle.

This 'picture' of 15 shows:

3 × 5 = 15

and 5 × 3 = 15

3 is a **factor** of 15

and 5 is a factor of 15

15 is a **multiple** of 3

and 15 is a multiple of 5.

- Explain, to a partner, what your rectangle shows.
- Draw your rectangle pattern or cut it from square dotty paper.
- Write what your rectangle shows alongside it.

- Make six different rectangle numbers and record your results.

  On page 8, 'Building with numbers', you found out about **prime** numbers.

- What is the connection between rectangle numbers and prime numbers? Write down your findings.

Y 9 ALGEBRA – C

... Shapes and numbers

... square numbers

- peg board
- coloured pegs

☐ Make this pattern on a peg board:

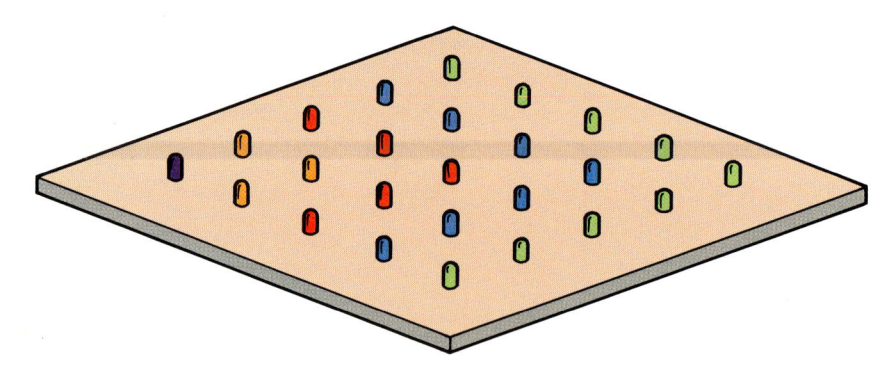

1. How many pegs do you need to make each square?
2. How many of each colour do you need?
3. How many more pegs would you need for the next square?

■ Check your prediction.

☐ Continue your pattern up to the tenth square.

Some square patterns can be made into a rectangle pattern:

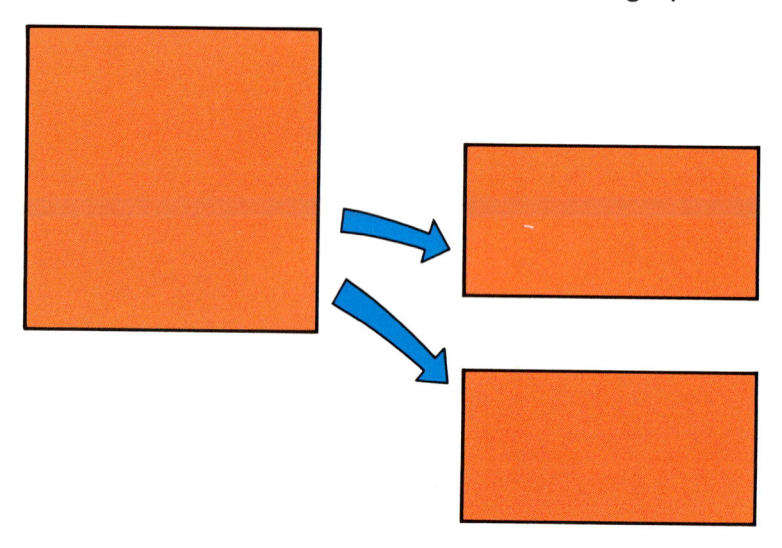

☐ Which numbers could this square pattern be?

Make a list of these numbers.

☐ What are the sides of the rectangle for each of your square patterns?

... Shapes and numbers

... triangle numbers

✓ 'Martello Tower'

■ Draw some staircases like these.

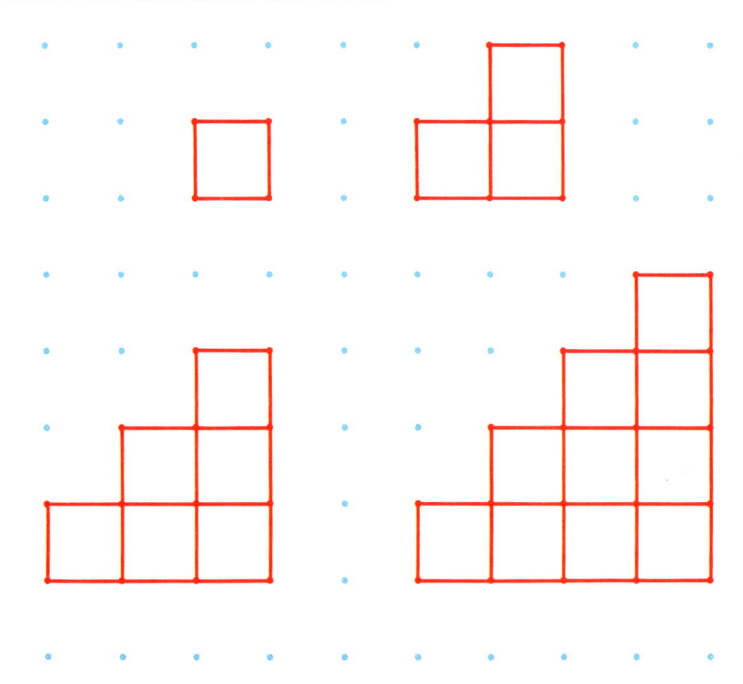

[1] What number pattern do you get?

☐ Write the numbers and continue the sequence.

■ Repeat the activities above using isometric dotty instead of square dotty paper:

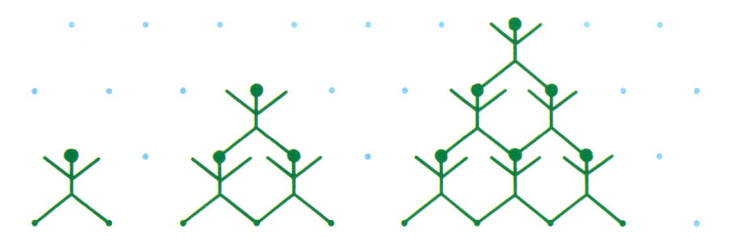

Your number pattern is the same as one of those on page 10, '. . . the number line'.

[2] Which one?

■ Can you explain why?

☐ Martello Tower'   ■ Play the adventure game 'Martello Tower'.

You will find that you need triangle numbers to escape!

Y 9 ALGEBRA – C

... Shapes and numbers

... squares and triangles

This square number can be split into two triangle numbers.

One is a bit bigger than the other.

In this diagram:

25 → 10 and 15

■ Using square dotty paper, cut out two, five by five squares like the one in the diagram.

■ Cut one of them into two triangles.

■ Display your results.

■ Do the same for the first ten square numbers.

■ Display your results so that you can spot any patterns more easily.

☐ Write about any patterns that you find.

[1] What would happen with a 20 by 20 square?

■ Check your prediction.

■ Explain your findings to a partner.

■ Can you convince them?

... Shapes and numbers

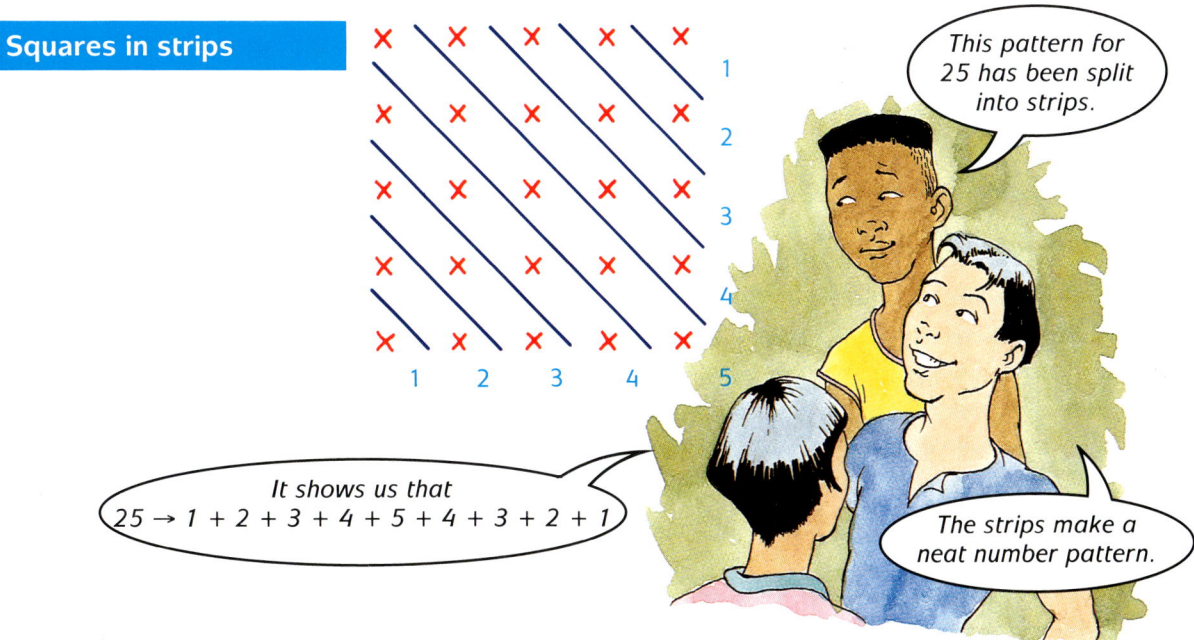

Squares in strips

This pattern for 25 has been split into strips.

It shows us that 25 → 1 + 2 + 3 + 4 + 5 + 4 + 3 + 2 + 1

The strips make a neat number pattern.

■ Do you get this pattern with other square numbers?

☐ Check some until you are sure.

☐ What is 1 + 2 + 3 . . . 20 + . . . 2 + 1?

Now compare: 15 → 5 × 3 → 1 + 2 + 3 + 3 + 3 + 2 + 1

with: 16 → 4 × 4 → . . .

■ In your group, discuss what you can see in these patterns.

■ Compare some more rectangle and square numbers.

☐ Write down any patterns that you notice.

Y 9 ALGEBRA – C

... Shapes and numbers

Staircases

✓ Multilink

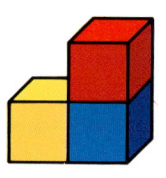

This staircase has two steps.

1. How many bricks does it need?

■ Make a staircase with three steps.
2. How many bricks does it need?

■ Repeat for four, five and six steps.
3. How many bricks do you need for each one?

□ Is there a pattern?

Describe it in words.

Now let's look at some different staircases.

This one goes up and down.

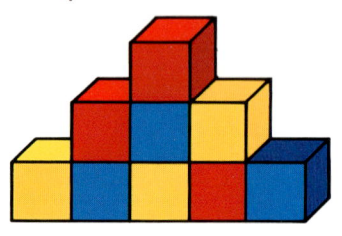

□ In your group build some staircases that go up and down.
4. How many bricks do you need for each of these staircases?
■ Describe any patterns you find.

I've built this staircase – it's in 3-D

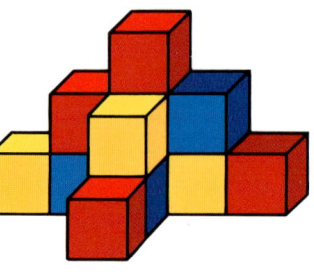

Does it have steps in the front and at the back?

■ Describe the patterns you find building 3-D staircases.

Unit 3 Sequences and mappings

Describing sequences

On page 10 there is a sequence or string of numbers –

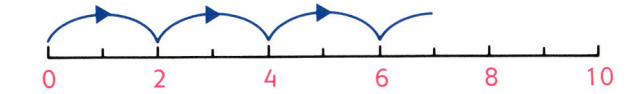

```
0   2   4   6   8   10
```

You could describe it by saying something like – 'Starting at zero, add two each time . . .'

1. What number sequence do you get?

2. How would you describe this sequence in words?

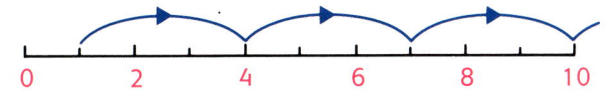

```
0   2   4   6   8   10
```

3. What number do you get?

   Write down the first eight . . .

4. Do the same for these:

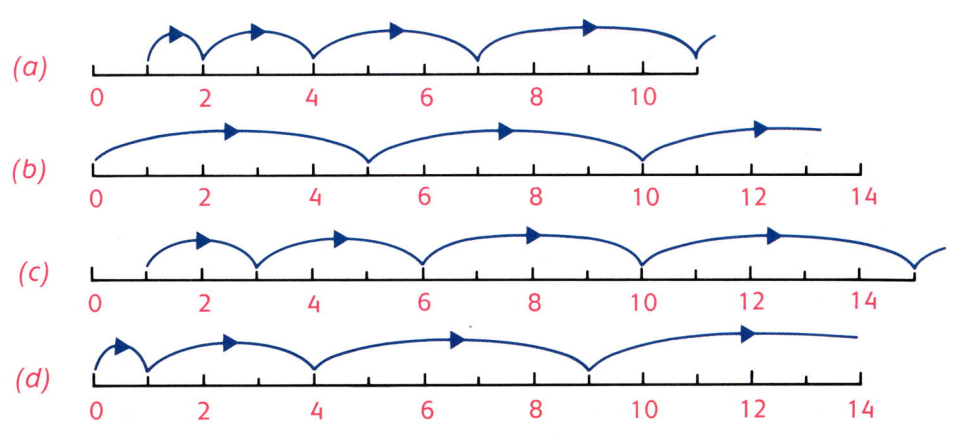

   (a)
   ```
   0   2   4   6   8   10
   ```

   (b)
   ```
   0   2   4   6   8   10   12   14
   ```

   (c)
   ```
   0   2   4   6   8   10   12   14
   ```

   (d)
   ```
   0   2   4   6   8   10   12   14
   ```

   The last three have special names.

5. What are they?

- Work with a partner.
- Each write down a number pattern.
- On a different page or sheet write down its description in words.
- Swap with your partner.
- Write down her sequence. Were you right?
- Play this three or four times.

Y 9 ALGEBRA – C

... Sequences and mappings

Calculator sequences

■ Look at this calculator sequence.

`2` `+` `2` `=` `+` `2` `=` `+` `2` `=` ...

Do we need to use the `=` button each time?

1. What sequence does this give?

   Write down the first ten terms.

   These are the even numbers four, six, eight, ten ...

■ Look at this sequence:

`1` `×` `5` `=` `×` `5` `=` `×` `5` `=` ...

2. What sequence does this give?
3. What is this sequence called?
4. What keys would give these number sequences?

   (a) 5 10 15 20 ...

   (b) 9 8 7 6 ...

   (c) 32 16 8 4 ...

5. Write down the next four terms for each one.

■ In your group, work out how you would get:

   (a) multiples of four – 4, 8, 12 ...

   (b) odd numbers – 1, 3, 5 ...

   (c) powers of three – 3, 9, 27 ...

   (d) square numbers – 1, 4, 9 ...

Try this key sequence.
`8` `√` `√` `√` `√`

What numbers do you get?

What number will you end with?

■ Can you explain why?

... Sequences and mappings

Rules for sequences

Some calculators, particularly graphic calculators, allow you to place numbers in memories called A, B, C ... and so on.

■ If you have a Texas TI 81, try this:

Press `5` `STO▶` `A` `ENTER`

■ Now try pressing `2` `STO▶` `A` `ENTER`

[1] What do you get?

■ Explore what else you could do to A.

■ Try finding $A + 1$, $3A + 2$, ...

■ Place 3 in memory N by pressing

`3` `STO▶` `N` `ENTER`

■ Work out $\dfrac{N(N + 1)}{2}$ by pressing

`ALPHA` `N` `(` `ALPHA` `N` `+` `1` `)` `÷` `2` `ENTER`

■ Try placing different numbers in N and finding $\dfrac{N(N + 1)}{2}$

☐ Put your results in a table

N	1	2	3	4	5	6	7	8
$\dfrac{N(N+1)}{2}$			6					

[2] Do you recognise the sequence of numbers?

■ Explore the rules $N \longrightarrow 2N$
$N \longrightarrow N^2$

[3] What sequences of numbers do they make?

[4] What rules make these sequences?

(a) 3, 5, 7, 9, 11 ...

(b) 1, 8, 27 ...

(c) 0, 3, 6, 9 ...

(d) 4, 7, 10, 13 ...

Y 9 ALGEBRA – C

... Sequences and mappings

Flowcharts

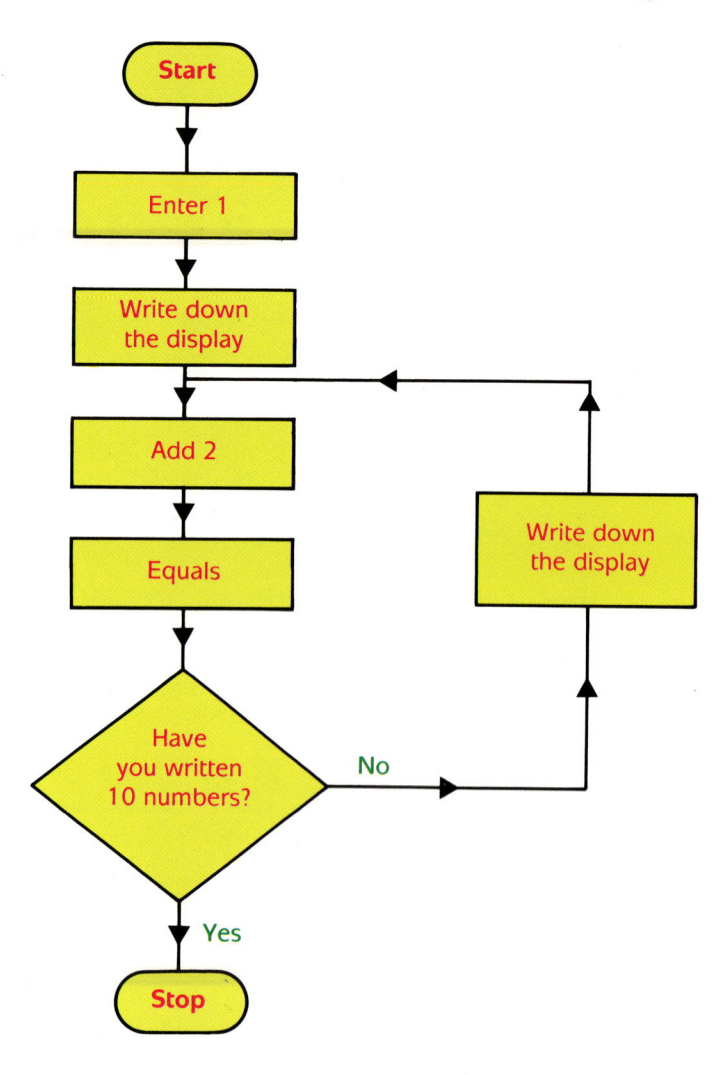

```
Start
  ↓
Enter 1
  ↓
Write down the display
  ↓
Add 2  ←──────────┐
  ↓               │
Equals            │
  ↓               │
Have you written  │
10 numbers? ──No──→ Write down the display
  ↓ Yes
Stop
```

■ Follow this flowchart on a calculator.

1. What is this number sequence called?

2. Change the flowchart to give

    (a) the first eight <u>even</u> numbers,

    (b) multiples of six.

3. Draw a flowchart to give

    (a) 6000   600   60   6

    (b) 8   12   18   27   40.5

    (c) 1   −2   4   −8   16   −32.

... Sequences and mappings

Fibonacci

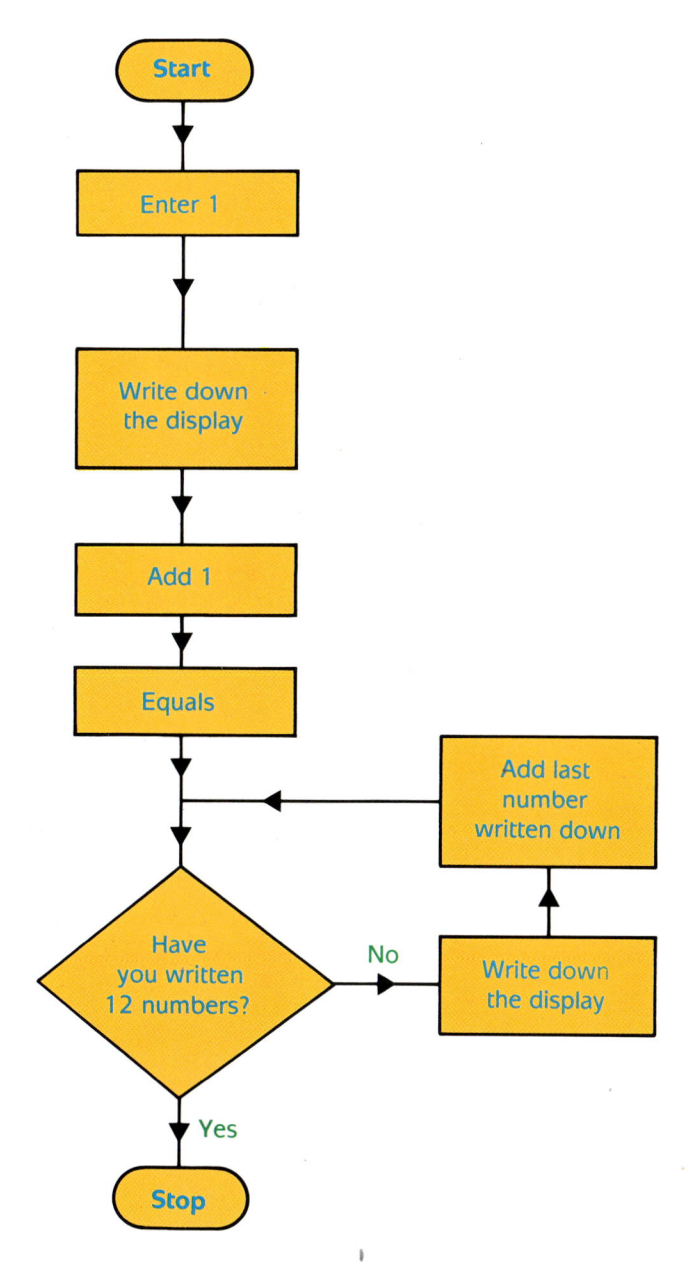

```
Start
  ↓
Enter 1
  ↓
Write down the display
  ↓
Add 1
  ↓
Equals
  ↓
Have you written 12 numbers? --No--> Write down the display --> Add last number written down --> (back to Have you written 12 numbers?)
  ↓ Yes
Stop
```

- Follow this flowchart.

  *It gives the **Fibonacci** sequence, named after a mathematician who wrote about it nearly 800 years ago.*

- In your group, try starting with different numbers.
- What do you notice?

Y 9 ALGEBRA – C

... Sequences and mappings

Calculator mappings

G2c, 2t

Start with any number on your calculator.

Press these buttons . . . × 2 − 1 =

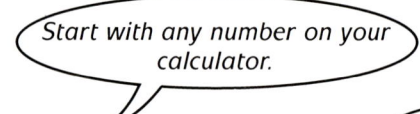

What number do you get?

☐ Choose another number to start. Predict the answer. Now press the calculator buttons. How good was your prediction?

☐ Start with different numbers.

☐ Record your results in a table like this:

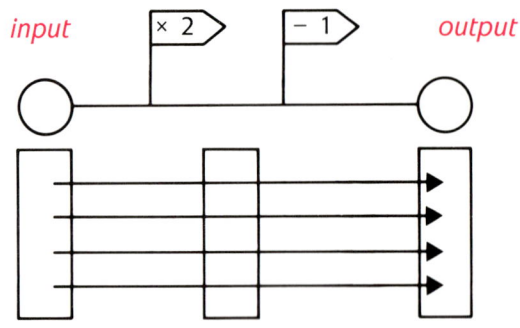

input × 2 − 1 output

G2c, 2t

1 Each of the results below was produced by a different sequence of buttons.

What sequence of buttons produced each of the results?

	input	output		input	output
(a)	2 → 6		(b)	3 → 8	
	5 → 15			7 → 16	
	3 → 9			2 → 6	
	7 → 21			1 → 4	

	input	output		input	output
(c)	1 → 9		(d)	2 → 4	
	6 → 24			5 → 13	
	3 → 15			1 → 1	
	0 → 6			4 → 10	

■ Try to explain how your group found the sequences of buttons.

☐ Make up a sequence of two operations. On a separate piece of paper, write down a list of inputs and the outputs.

☐ Swap lists of inputs and outputs and find the sequence of buttons your partner used.

... Sequences and mappings

Working from the answer ...

1. What sequence of buttons on a calculator produced these results?

input	output
3	5
10	12
2	4
7	9

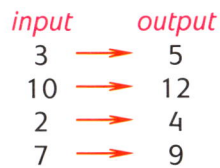

   *The reverse of an operation is called the **inverse**.*

2. What buttons would reverse these results? So that:

input	output
5	3
12	10
4	2
9	7

3. In each of the following, give the sequence of buttons which gives you the operation and its inverse.

   (a)

   operation

input	output
6	1
10	5
8	3
12	7

   inverse

input	output
1	6
5	10
3	8
7	12

   (b)

input	output
2	6
5	15
1	3
4	12

input	output
6	2
15	5
3	1
12	4

*So, the **inverse** of × 2 is ÷ 2 and the **inverse** of + 3 is − 3.*

■ How could you decribe what you've found out?

When you add, the inverse is ...

Yes, and when you subtract, the inverse is ...

Y 9 ALGEBRA – C

... Sequences and mappings

There and back again

1 Write down the rule for each of these by finding what operation goes into each flag.

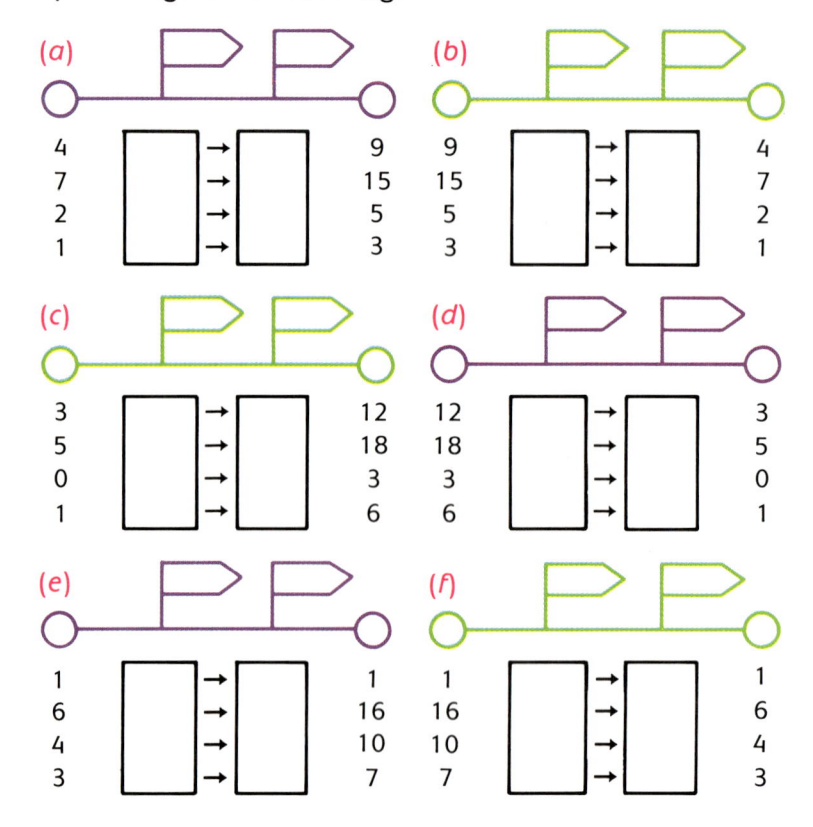

(a)
4	→	9
7	→	15
2	→	5
1	→	3

(b)
9	→	4
15	→	7
5	→	2
3	→	1

(c)
3	→	12
5	→	18
0	→	3
1	→	6

(d)
12	→	3
18	→	5
3	→	0
6	→	1

(e)
1	→	1
6	→	16
4	→	10
3	→	7

(f)
1	→	1
16	→	6
10	→	4
7	→	3

■ Try to explain how your group found each rule.

If you multiply by 2 and add 1 . . .

. . . then the inverse is subtract 1 and divide by 2.

... Sequences and mappings

Mappings

✓ 2

The rule to change one set of numbers (the input) into another set of numbers (the output) can be shown in a number of different ways:

- as a sequence of buttons on a calculator

  [×] [2] [+] [1] [=]

- as data in a table

  3 → 7

  4 → 9

  5 → 11

- as an equation

  $y = 2x + 1$

or as a **mapping**

  $x \longrightarrow 2x + 1$

All these different ways show the rule 'multiply by two and add one'.

2

The mappings worksheet shows a number of different rules. Complete the worksheet by filling in the blank spaces. For example:

- calculator   [÷] [2] [+] [1] [=]

- data   2 → 2
                6 → ■

- equation $y = \dfrac{x}{2} + 1$

- mapping $x \longrightarrow$

It's divide by 2 and add 1.

... and 6 → 4.

So the mapping is $x \longrightarrow \dfrac{x}{2} + 1$.

1. Now complete the worksheet.

Y 9 ALGEBRA – C

... Sequences and mappings

Logo mappings

✓ L

L **LP** F2

■ Build this procedure in Logo.

There are two versions of the procedure.
Make sure you know which version your computer uses.

> To Map :x
> Pr P :x + 3
> end

■ Type Map 3 (and press return).

Logo will print 6

■ Input some more numbers (eg. Map 10 etc).

[1] What happens to the numbers you input?

■ Edit the procedure to change: $x + 3$ into $2 * :x + 3$

■ Type Map 5

■ Input some more numbers.

[2] What happens to the numbers you input?

[3] Here are a few Logo mappings.

Match each of them to one of the tables of inputs and outputs.

(a) $10 - :x$ (b) $3 * :x - 1$ (c) $:x/2$ (d) $5 * :x$

(i) 2 → 5   (ii) 6 → 30   (iii) 5 → 8
     5 → 14   5 → 25   8 → 14
    10 → 29   8 → 40   10 → 18
     4 → 11   2 → 10   3 → 4

(iv) 4 → 6   (v) 10 → 5
     9 → 1   2 → 1
     1 → 9   6 → 3
     6 → 4   12 → 6

■ One of the input/output tables remains.

Edit your procedure and find the mapping which produces these outputs.

[4] Write down the mapping you have found.

Let's try them on the computer.

... Sequences and mappings

Mapping games

Vijay secretly chooses one of these mappings.

$x \longrightarrow 2x - 1$

$x \longrightarrow x + 7$

$x \longrightarrow 3x + 1$

$x \longrightarrow 2x + 3$

$x \longrightarrow 3x - 2$

$x \longrightarrow 15 - x$

The rest of the group takes turns to suggest numbers as inputs.

- Vijay gave them each output.

The aim is to work out which mapping Vijay has choosen.

■ Play this game a few times in your group. Take turns to choose the mapping.

☐ You could also set this game up on a spreadsheet.

1 What is the least number of inputs necessary to make sure you know the mapping?

2 What are useful numbers to use as inputs?

☐ Are some of the functions easier to discover than others?

■ Now try thinking of your own mappings.

LN S3

One person writes down a mapping without anyone else seeing.

The other members of the group have to work out the mapping as before.

Try including dividing, brackets . . . and so on.

- You might need to agree rules so that the mappings are not too complicated!

Y 9 ALGEBRA − C

Unit 4 Numbers from patterns

Sending signals

✓ Library

0   1   2   3

4   5

■ Look at the pictures above.

Try to work out what the code is.

■ Work with a partner.

Stand next to each other and use your arms to continue the counting pattern.

[1] What is the highest number you can signal with two people?

Now try it with three people.

As the numbers grow larger you will probably want to stop signalling the numbers and use your own way of recording.

[2] How many people do you need to do all numbers up to 100? . . . 1000?

Braille

Braille is the system of writing used by blind people.

☐ Who devised the system and when?

How does it work?

■ In your group, find out all you can about Braille.

Make a display for your classroom wall.

[1] In what ways are Braille and the signalling system on this page the same?

[2] What number system do computers use and why?

... Numbers from patterns

How many games?

Class 9C are doing PE in the gym. They are playing against each other in teams.

1. If there are four teams, how many different matches can they play?

2. What if there are five teams? . . . six teams?

■ Explain your answers to your partner.

Describe any patterns you find.

3. Use your pattern to predict how many games you would have with:
   - 10 teams
   - 20 teams
   - 100 teams.

Knockout

Later in the year the children arrange a knockout competition for unihoc (indoor hockey). There are 32 forms in the school and each form enters a team.

1. How many matches are there in the first round?

□ Draw up a poster to show all the matches up to the final.

2. What number pattern do you get here?

3. How many rounds are there?

4. What happens if you have 40 teams in the competition?

Y 9 ALGEBRA − C

... Numbers from patterns

Hexagon numbers

✓ counters or coins
hexagon paper

Kelly tried to make this 'flower' with some coins.

- Discuss whether the six coins fit exactly around the middle coin.
- Now make the pattern for yourself. Were you correct?

Kelly placed another layer around her flower:

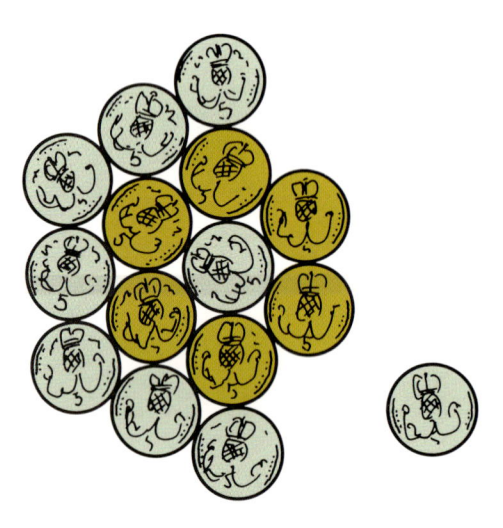

1. How many coins did she need to surround the gold coins?
2. How many coins did she use all together?
- Add more layers and continue her number pattern.
- Try to predict how many you will need.
- Record your results on hexagon paper.

. . . Numbers from patterns

More coins

✓ counters or coins

Scott's coins will fit together to make triangle patterns.

■ Make some triangles and record your results.

Scott drew the circles using compasses on plain paper.

☐ Try to draw the pattern on plain paper. This diagram will help <u>you</u> get started.

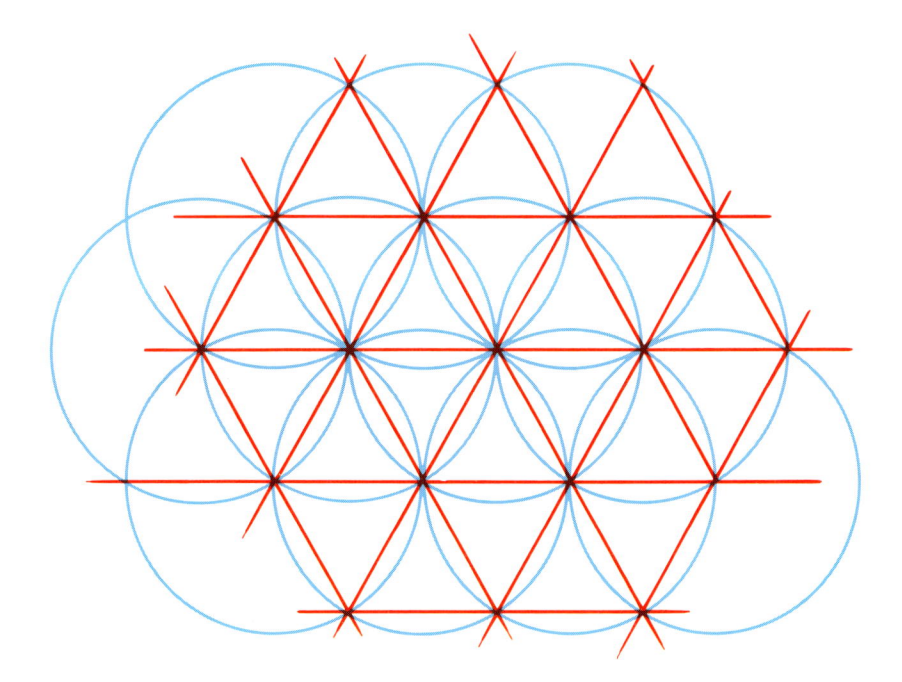

☐ If you find it difficult, isometric dotty paper will help you choose the centres for your circles.

Y 9 ALGEBRA – C

... Numbers from patterns

Patterns in 3-D

G3c, 3t

centicubes or Unifix

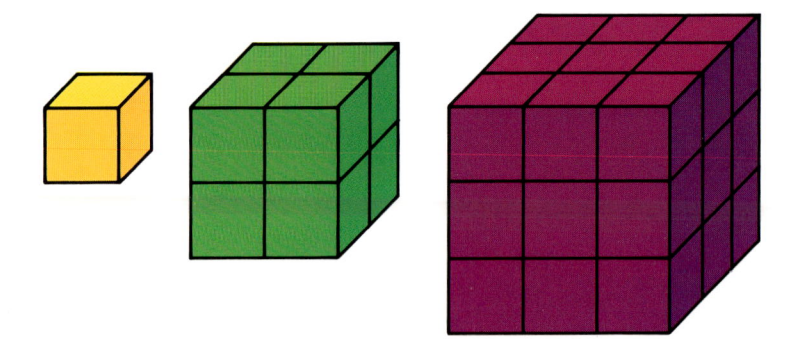

■ Build this set of cubes.

[1] How many small cubes do you need for each?

2 × 2 × 2 can be written 2^3 and is spoken 'two cubed'

■ Can you see why?

Try to explain your answer to your partner.

[2] What does 'three cubed' mean?

[3] How many is 3^3?

[4] How many is 4^3?
... 5^3?

■ Use a calculator to check your calculations.

☐ If you use a scientific calculator, find the key [y^x]

Key in [4] [y^x] [3] [=]

[5] What is the answer?

■ Experiment with the [y^x] key. What is happening?

[6] What is 11^3?
... 20^3?

[7] Find the missing number:

$7^3 = ?$

$?^3 = 512$

$?^3 = 2197$

[8] Which cube number is closest to 1000?
... 500 000?
... a million?

... Numbers from patterns

3-D triangles

✓ tennis balls
  marbles or conkers

Scott looked at triangles again.

This time he built triangular pyramids using tennis balls.

1. How many did he need for each pyramid?

2. How many extra tennis balls did he need each time?

■ Continue the sequence for the next four pyramids.

3. When you put a lot of spheres in a container what arrangement do they make?

4. How many other spheres does one sphere touch?

In 'Hexagon numbers' on page 30, you found that circles and hexagons made similar patterns.

5. Can you think of an example in nature where '3-D hexagons' are packed tightly like the balls above?

☐ With a partner, build some pyramids using cubes.

☐ What number patterns do you get?

Y 9 ALGEBRA – C

... Numbers from patterns

Curve stitching

✓ ☐ MicroSmile 1: 'Rose'

This diagram shows a half-finished picture made by Louis threading cotton from each hole to every other hole.

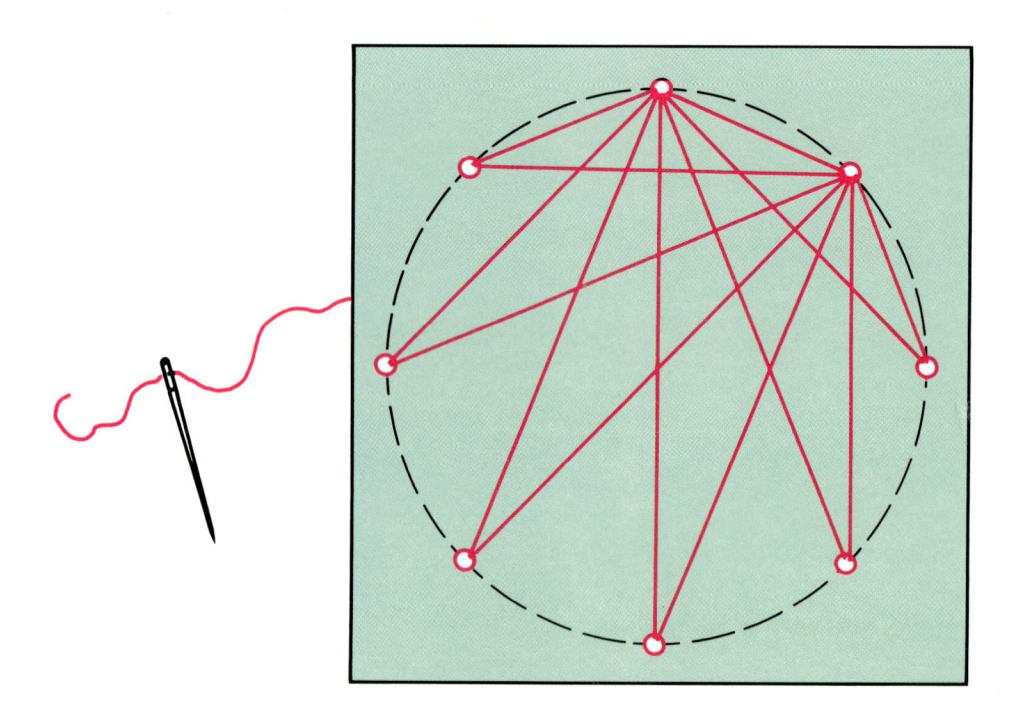

☐ Draw your own circle and copy the diagram.

☐ Finish the picture, showing what Louis should obtain.

1. How many lines are there?

   If you find this question difficult, try an easier picture.

2. Work out how many lines you get for:

   – four holes

   – five holes

   – six holes.

■ What do you notice?

■ Use the computer program 'Rose'.

☐ MicroSmile 1: 'Rose'

... Numbers from patterns

Tiles

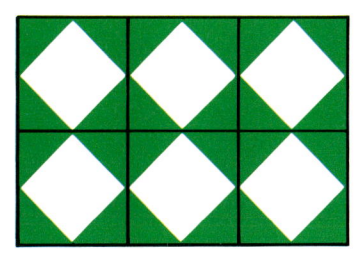

The diagram shows six tiles from a popular range sold in a DIY store. Each tile is 10 cm square.

☐ Draw a single tile full size.

The area of a tile is 10 × 10 = 100 cm^2

■ Explain to your partner, a way of showing that the area of the white part = 50 cm^2

■ Measure the side of the white square.

☐ Write down the length of the side in cm.

■ Use your calculator to find the area of the square.

■ Did you get exactly 50 cm^2?

Discuss how you could get a more accurate result.

1. Find the missing numbers:

   $a \times a = 169$

   $b \times b = 289$

   $c \times c = 441$

Ten squared is 100.

Yes, and you can use this button on the calculator to find square roots √‾ .

So 10 is the square root of 100.

Estimating squares

This is a game for two or three people.

Take it in turn to write down a two- or three-digit number.

All players then guess its square root.

Find out who is the closest with a calculator.

When you are good at it, try a harder version by choosing four-digit numbers.

Y 9 ALGEBRA – C

Unit 5 Exploring numbers

Balancing acts

- coat-hanger or thin strips of wood

You may have used a balance or 'equaliser' like this:

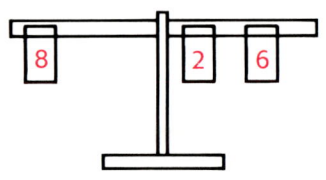

[8] | [2][6]

This one balances because 8 = 2 + 6

1. What must ? be to make this one balance?

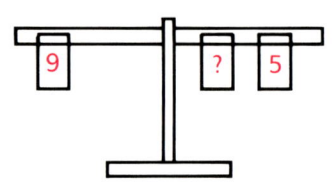

[9] | [?][5]

2. Make the following balances by finding out what ? must be.

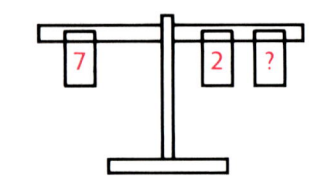

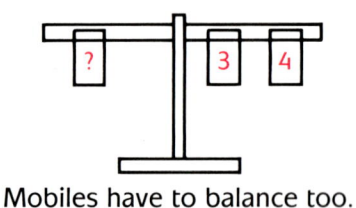

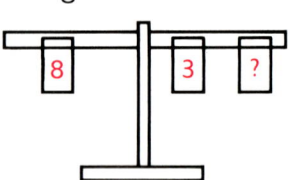

[7][2][?]   [?][3][4]   [8][3][?]

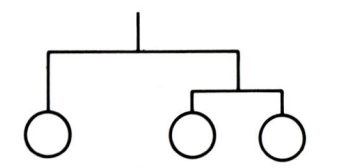

Mobiles have to balance too.

■ Now it's your turn to make a mobile with your partner.

Use a coat-hanger, or ruler, or thin strips of wood.

This mobile balances.

Make it to check that it does.

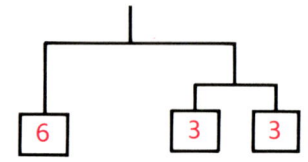

[6] [3][3]

3. Make the following mobiles balance by finding the missing numbers in each case.

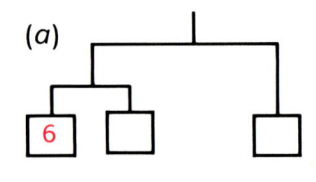

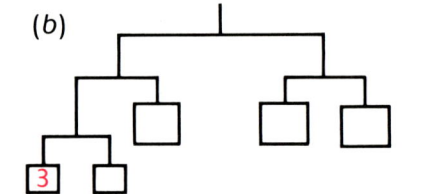

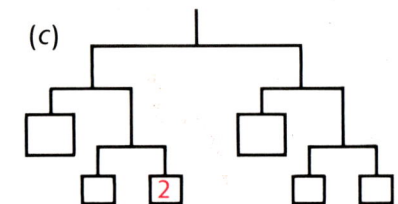

(a) [6] [ ] [ ]

(b) [3] [ ] [ ] [ ]

(c) [ ] [2] [ ] [ ]

■ With your partner, design and make a mobile to hang in your classroom or bedroom at home.

... Exploring numbers

Number squares

[S] LN S2, S3

■ Use a spreadsheet to construct some of these number squares.

	1	2	3	4	5
1	2	3	4	5	6
2	3	4	5	6	7
3	4	5	6	7	8
4	5	6	7	8	9
5	6	7	8	9	10

	5	4	3	2	1
1	6	5	4	3	2
2	7	6	5	4	3
3	8	7	6	5	4
4	9	8	7	6	5
5	10	9	8	7	6

	5	4	3	2	1
5	10	9	8	7	6
4	9	8	7	6	5
3	8	7	6	5	4
2	7	6	5	4	3
1	6	5	4	3	2

	1	2	3	4	5
1	1	2	3	4	5
2	2	4	6	8	10
3	3	6	9	12	15
4	4	8	12	16	20
5	5	10	15	20	25

	1	2	3	4	5
5	5	10	15	20	25
4	4	8	12	16	20
3	3	6	9	12	15
2	2	4	6	8	10
1	1	2	3	4	5

☐ Write down how you constructed each number square.

■ Make up a number square of your own.

Give it to your partner to construct using a spreadsheet.

Y 9 ALGEBRA – C

... Exploring numbers

Investigating growth patterns

Here is a series of pictures of a 'fish'.
It is growing systematically.

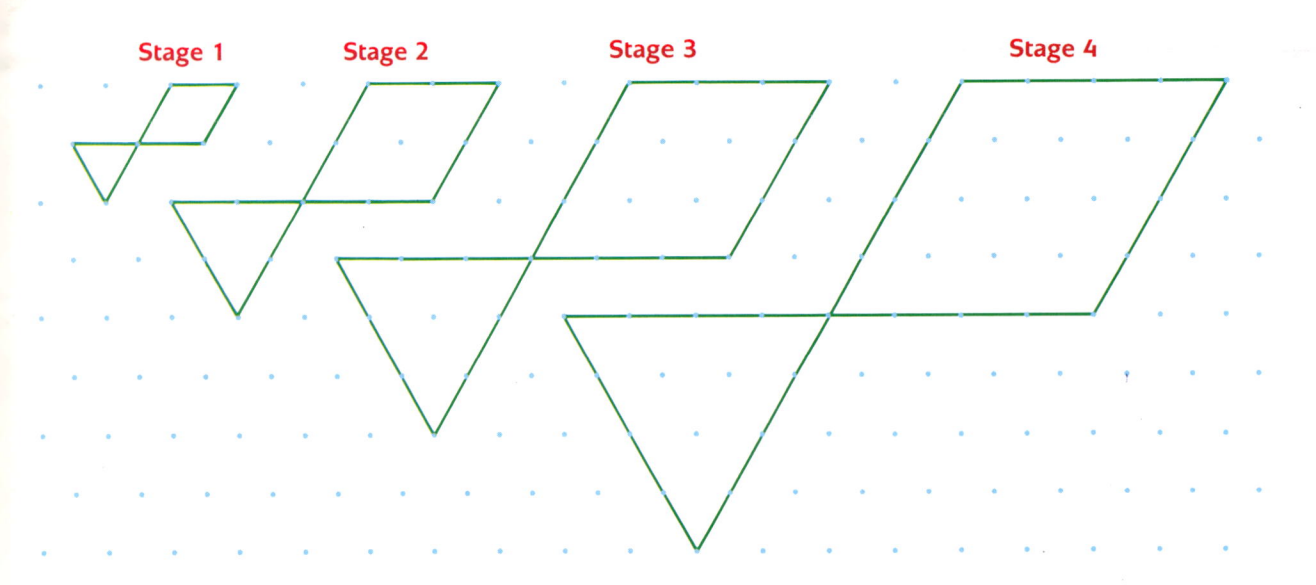

Stage 1   Stage 2   Stage 3   Stage 4

■ Measure how it grows in at least three different ways.

Stage of growth	1	2	3	4	10
Perimeter of the fish	7	14	21		
Number of spots inside the fish's tail	0	0	1		
Number of spots inside the fish's body	0	1	4		
Total area of the fish (triangular units)	3	12	27		

☐ Complete the stages of results up to ten stages of growth.

■ Look for patterns in your table and try to describe them to your partner.

■ What can you say about the fish after 100 stages of growth?
Try to convince the rest of your group!

☐ Can you draw graphs and find formulae to describe what you have found out?

☐ Make a group display of your results.

... Exploring numbers

■ Here are some ideas to start you off. Try some of these and then invent your own.

You don't have to make your shapes look like animals.

I could count areas, perimeters, corners, dots, surface areas, volumes . . . the possibilities are endless.

Y 9 ALGEBRA – C

... Exploring numbers

Formulae for perimeters

G4C, 4T

Starting point

For this rectangle:
- the length is 6
- the width is 4
- the perimeter is 20

Draw some more rectangles.

Explore the relationship between the length, width and perimeter.

Conclusions

perimeter = p
length = l
width = w
For my rectangle
p = 2l + 2w

Conclusions

perimeter = p
length = l
width = w
For my rectangle
p = 2(l + w)

This is the work of two pupils

■ Discuss these conclusions in your group.

1. Which conclusion do you think is right, or are they both correct?

■ Convince your group.

2. Find formulae for the perimeters of:
   - squares
   - parallelograms
   - and so on . . .

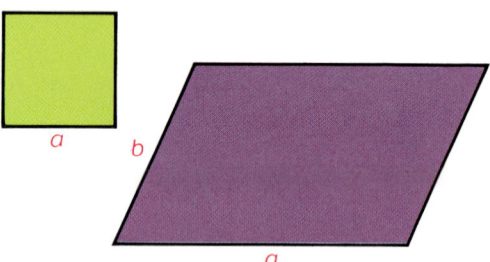

3. Are there formulae for areas of:
   - squares
   - rectangles
   - parallelograms?

4. Are there formulae for volumes of:
   - cubes
   - cuboids?

■ Discuss questions 3 and 4 in your group.

Try to arrive at a formula for the area and volume of each shape.

G4C, 4T

... Exploring numbers

Explaining the results

The starting point:

> **Nails**
>
> Make a shape on a pinboard with an elastic band.
>
> This band touches eight nails.
>
> Inside the shape are two nails.
>
> The area is 5 cm².
>
> Explore the relationship between the number of nails and the area.

This is my work.

What's the total number of nails?

The total number of nails is those on the inside and those touching the rubber band.

Number of nails inside band = I
Total number of nails = t
Area in square cm = A

For any shape with 2I
$$\frac{t}{2} = A$$

For any shape with 3I
$$\frac{t+1}{2} = A$$

For any shape with 1I
$$\frac{t-1}{2} = A$$

For any shape with no nails inside
$$\frac{t-2}{2} = A$$

☐ Do you agree with the conclusion?

I'm going to try some shapes

Let's start with one with two nails inside.

Yes, but how will we know it always works?

■ Convince your partner that this formula:
$$A = \frac{(I - 2) + t}{2}$$

gives the area for any shape.

Y 9 ALGEBRA – C

... Exploring numbers

Puzzling words

You might have seen puzzles like this before.

```
   A A
 + B B
 -----
 C B C
```

C must be 1.

To solve this puzzle, replace the letters with digits to make the addition correct.

Why?

Because when you add A + B you can't carry more than 1 into the next column.

I'm going to check that.

☐ Use a table like this to keep track of the possible values for the letters:

	0	1	2	3	4	5	6	7	8	9
A		x								
B		x								
C		x								
D	x	✓	x	x	x	x	x	x	x	x

A could be zero.

Yes, but having the number 00 is silly!

So B is not 0 either.

	0	1	2	3	4	5	6	7	8	9
A	x	x								
B	x	x								
C	x	✓	x	x	x	x	x	x	x	x

A could be anything.

No, A + B = 11.

So we could try A as 2, and B as . . .

■ Now see if you can solve the puzzle.

☐ Write down your solution.

■ Is there more than one solution?

... Exploring numbers

☐ Now try this

```
    I T
+   T O
-------
  T O T
```

☐ Make up some puzzles like this.

Swap puzzles with your partner.

Try to solve your partner's puzzles.

T must be 1 this time.

■ This puzzle is much harder

```
  NINE
− FOUR
------
  FIVE
```

There are 72 different ways of solving this problem!

Let's see how many we can find.

☐ Now try these

```
  FORTY
+   TEN
    TEN
-------
  SIXTY
```

```
  HOCUS
+ POCUS
-------
  PRESTO
```

■ These puzzles are additions in the Hindi number script.

They are very difficult to solve. Try them.

१२२५
+ १२२५

९५८२६

१६२३३
+ ६२२९३

९२५९४६

☐ Can you make a puzzle like this in another number script?
(eg. Arabic, Bengali or Chinese?)

Y 9 ALGEBRA − C

Unit 6 Moving shapes

Moving houses

✓ mirror

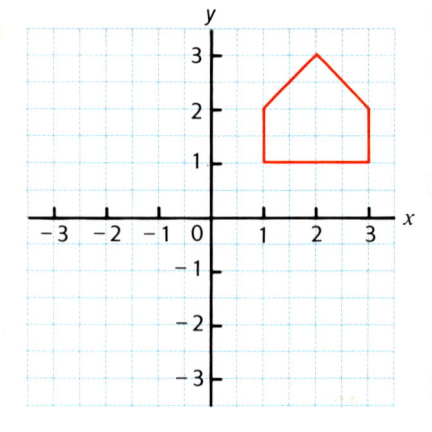

[1] Write down the coordinates of the corners of the house.

■ Add two to each *x*-coordinate.

(eg. (1, 1) becomes (3, 1))

[2] Write down the set of coordinates.

□ Plot these on a grid marked −10 to +10 on each axis.

[3] What happens to the house?

■ In each of the following,
  − start with the original coordinates
  − write down the new coordinates
  − plot the points and describe what happens to the house.

[4] Subtract five from the *x*-coordinate.

(e.g. (1, 1) becomes (−4, 1))

[5] Add three to the *y*-coordinate.

((1, 1) becomes (1, 4))

[6] Subtract four from the *y*-coordinate.

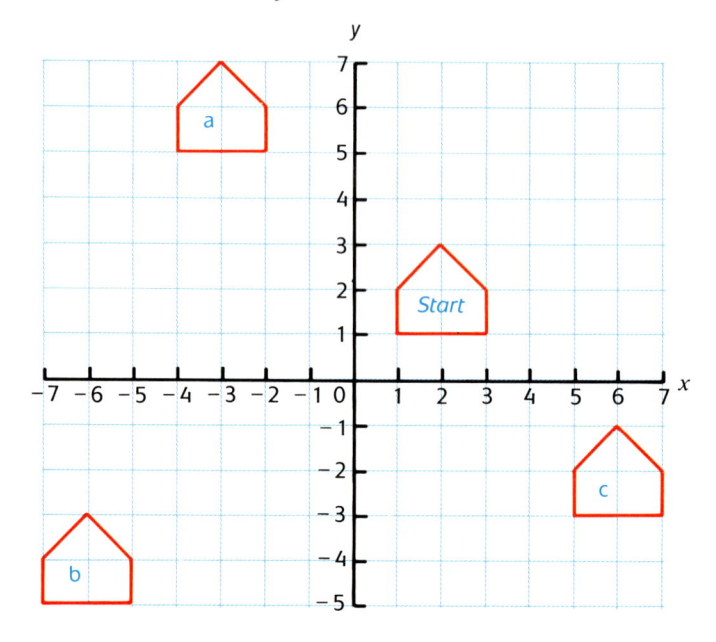

[7] Describe how to move the house from its starting position to each of these positions.

... Moving shapes

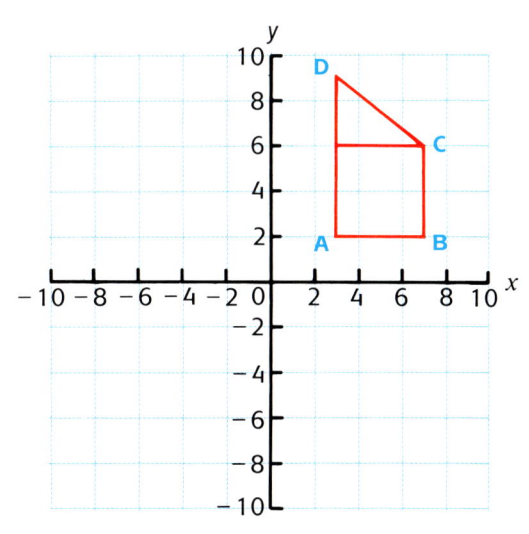

■ Put a mirror along the y-axis.

□ On a grid like the one above, draw the shape and its reflection.

8 What happens to the coordinates of the corners **A, B, C, D**?

□ On another grid, draw a different shape.
Reflect it in the y-axis.

9 Find out what happens to the coordinates.

■ Can you explain what happens?

□ Now try reflecting your shapes in the x-axis.

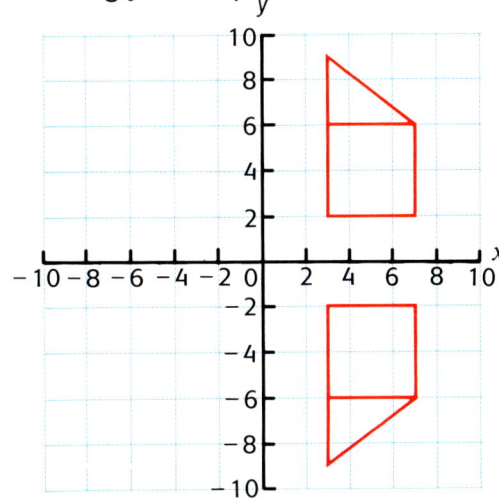

10 What happens to the coordinates?

■ Explain clearly to your partner.

LP C1

Y 9 ALGEBRA − C

... Moving shapes

Changing shapes

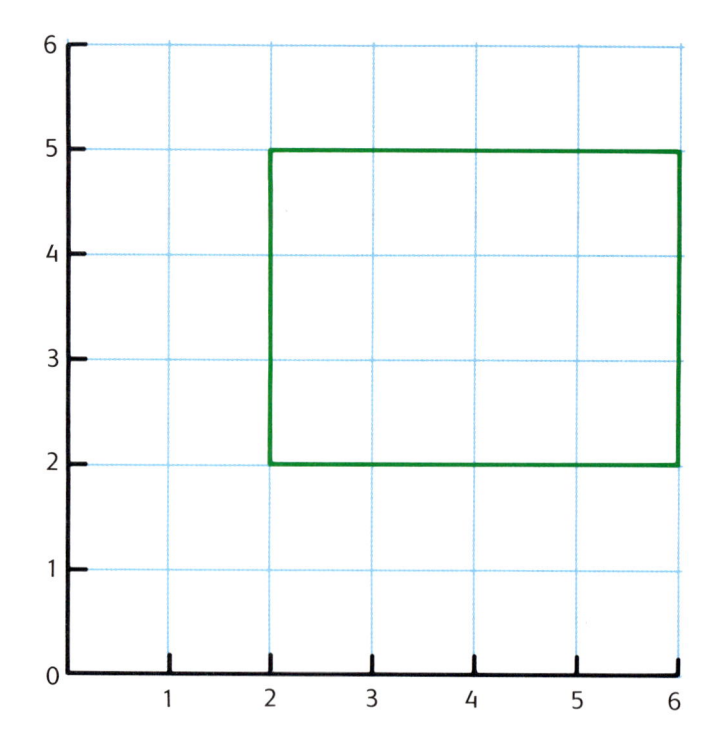

1. Which of these coordinates are the corners of the shaded rectangle?

   (2, 2) (5, 2) (5, 4) (6, 2) (2, 5) (2, 6)

   On a copy of the 'Changing shapes' worksheet, plot the four corners and complete the shape on each of the grids.

   How does the rectangle change?

   Explain each clearly.

2. Which of the transformations

   (a) makes the rectangle bigger in all directions by the same amount − an **enlargement**

   (b) stretches the rectangle in one direction − a **one-way stretch**

   One of the transformations is called a **shear**.

3. Try to describe what you think a shear does to a square.

   On a second copy of the worksheet, make up a shape of your own and see how it changes.

... Moving shapes

Moving other shapes

○ mirror

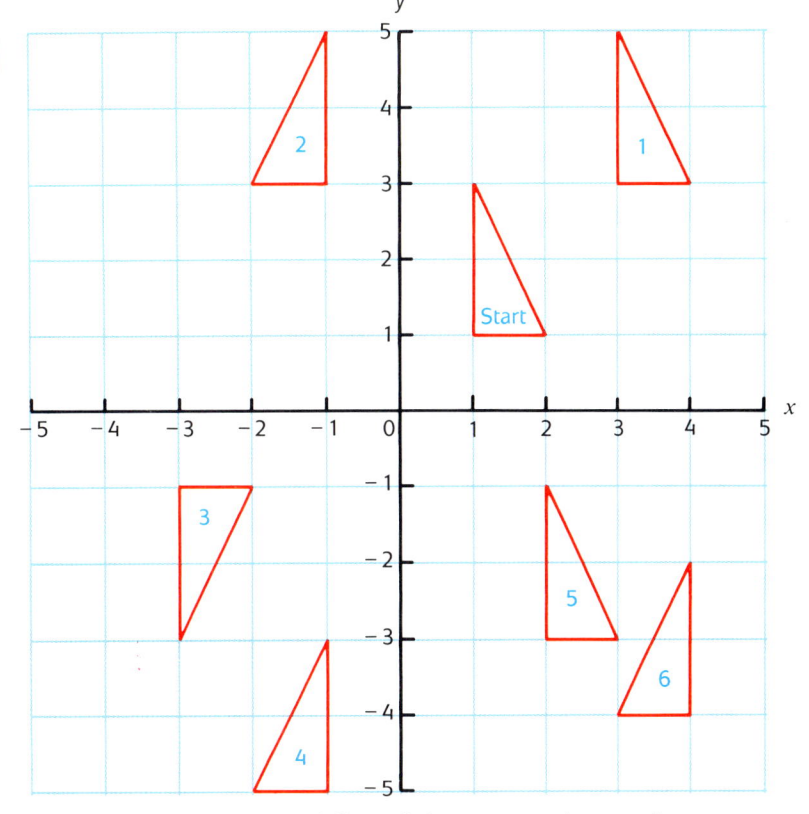

Here are descriptions of five of the moves shown above.

In each case the triangle starts in the same position.

1. Match the description to the finishing position.

   (a) Reflect in the *y*-axis, then subtract five from both coordinates.

   (b) Reflect in the *x*-axis, then subtract four from the *x*-coordinate.

   (c) Add two to both coordinates.

   (d) Reflect in the *y*-axis, then subtract six from the *y*-coordinate.

   (e) Add one to the *x*-coordinate, then subtract four from the *y*-coordinate.

2. One move has not been described.

   Write a suitable description for this move.

■ Set some puzzles like this for a partner.

Y 9 ALGEBRA – C

... Moving shapes

Shifting positions

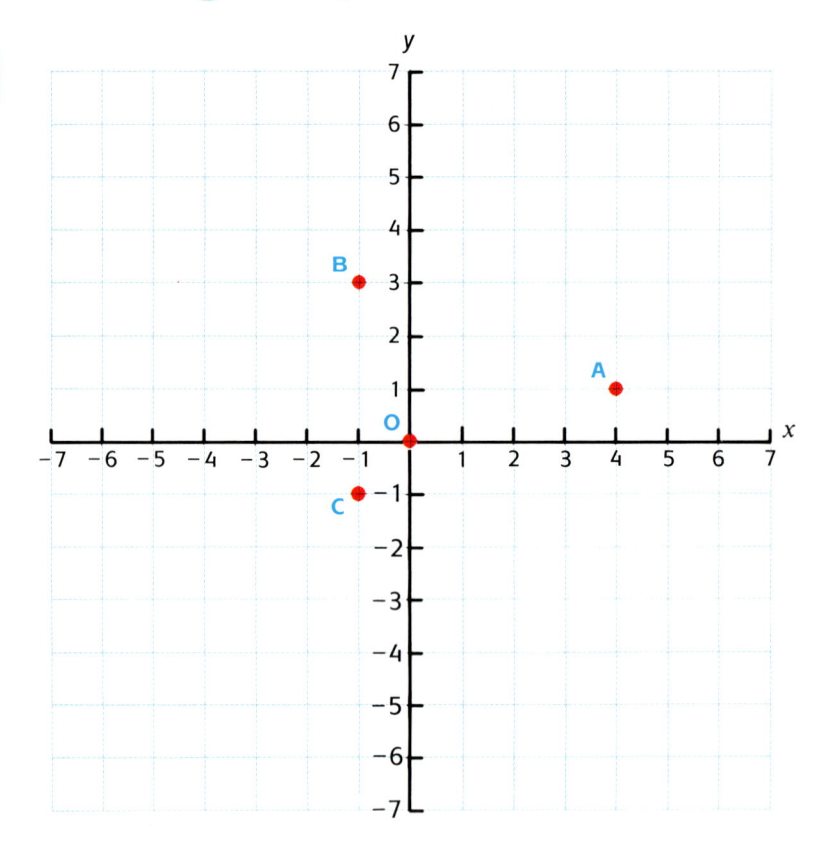

■ Place tracing paper over the grid above.

☐ Mark the points **O, A, B** and **C**.

■ Move your tracing of point **O**, two squares right and three squares up.

[1] What are the coordinates of all the points now?

■ Move **O** back to the original position.

■ Move **O** one square right, two squares down, three squares left and one square up.

[2] What are the coordinates of the points now?

■ Explore moving **O** various distances up, down, left and right.

[3] Try to explain what happens to the coordinates of the points.

Unit 7 Exploring graphs

Equations and graphs

✓ G5C, 5T
G or 🧮

[1] What are the coordinates of the points on this grid?

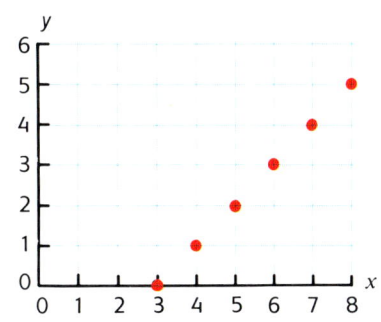

- Write the coordinates in a chart like this:

x	3
y	0

- Find a rule to link x and y.

- Find pairs of numbers that make the equation $y = x - 3$ true:

[2] What is the connection with your answers above?

- Find pairs of numbers that make the equation $y = x - 2$ true:

- Write the numbers in a table like the one above.

- Try negative numbers and decimals too.

- Plot the points from your table on a grid.

  Plot (2, 0) (5, 3) . . . and join up the points.

- Do the same for $y = x + 1$ and plot the points on the same graph.

G5C, 5T

L LP G1

S LN S1, S5

G LN P3

- Draw the graphs of these equations:

  $y = x;$ $y = x + 2;$ $y = x - 1$

[3] What can you say about the lines?

[4] Give the equations of three lines that are parallel to $y = 10 - x$

- Explore the graphs of equations such as:

  $y = 3x;$ $y = 10/x;$ $y = x^2$

Be careful, they are not all straight lines.

- Type your coordinates into a Logosheet and use the SG command to draw the scattergraph. Join up the points with the GRAPH command.

Y 9 ALGEBRA – C

. . . Exploring graphs

Plotting squares

G or [calculator]

S LN S1, S5

G LN P3

Four pegs form a square.

The side is length two.

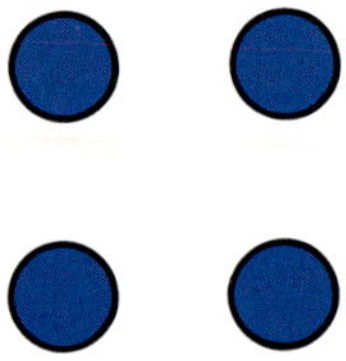

■ Explore what other numbers of pegs form squares.

A table of results would be helpful:

side	*number*
1	. . .
2	*4*
3	. . .
. . .	. . .

□ Plot a graph of side against number.

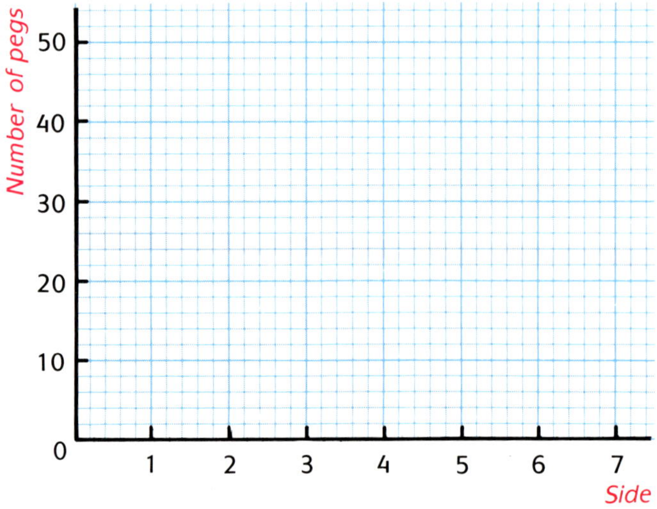

□ Use a graphic calculator, microcomputer, or pencil and paper to plot $y = x^2$

1 What do you notice?

□ In your group, explore the links between:

– the area of a circle and its radius

– the diagonal of a square and its area.

... Exploring graphs

Fixed perimeters

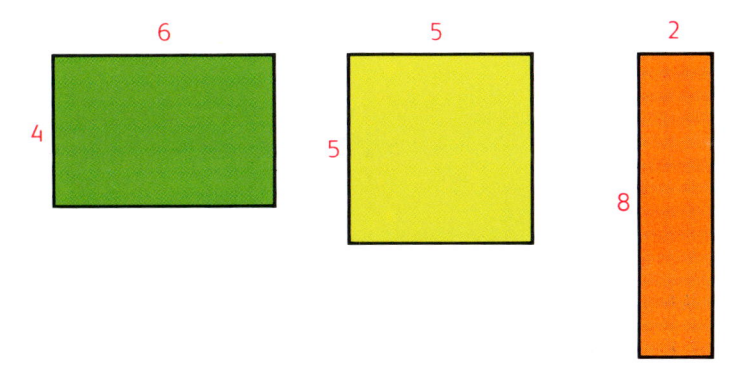

☑ G or 🖩

1. What do you notice about the perimeter of these rectangles?

   [rectangle 6 × 4]   [rectangle 5 × 5]   [rectangle 2 × 8]

   ☐ Draw some more rectangles with a perimeter of 20 cm.

   ☐ Plot a graph of length against width.

   [graph axes: Width (vertical) vs Length (horizontal)]

   ☐ Use a graphic calculator, microcomputer or pencil and paper to plot the graph of $y = 10 - x$.

2. What do you notice?

   ☐ In your group, explore the relationships between the perimeter and height of:

   – isosceles triangles

   – trapezia

   – parallelograms

   – regular pentagons.

   ☐ Now consider the links between:

   – the circumference of a circle and its diameter

   – the diagonal of a square and the side or perimeter.

Y 9 ALGEBRA – C

... Exploring graphs

Picturing graphs

G6C, 6T

LN P3 or

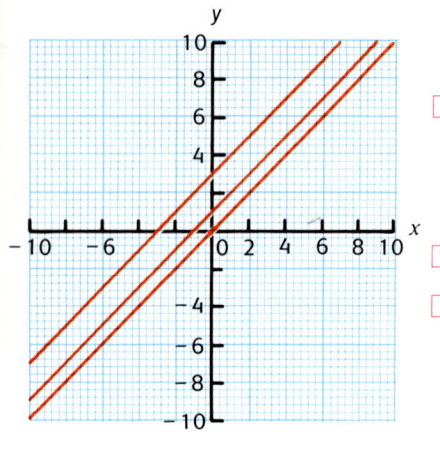

☐ On a graphic calculator, a microcomputer or on paper, plot the following graphs (set the ranges −10 to 10)

$y = x$

$y = x + 1$

$y = x + 2$

$y = x + 3$ ... and so on.

☐ Now try

$y = x - 1$

$y = x - 2$ ... and so on.

1 So for $y = x + c$, what does c tell you about the graph?

☐ On a new graph plot

$y = x$

$y = 2x$

$y = 3x$

and so on

and

$y = \frac{1}{2}x$ (or $y = 0.5x$)

$y = \frac{1}{3}x$

and so on.

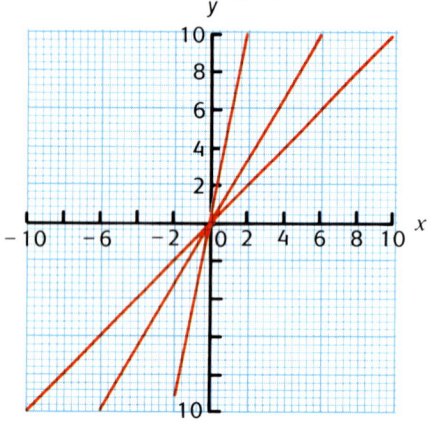

G6C, 6T

2 So for $y = mx$, what do you think m tells you about the graph?

3 How could you draw graphs like these?

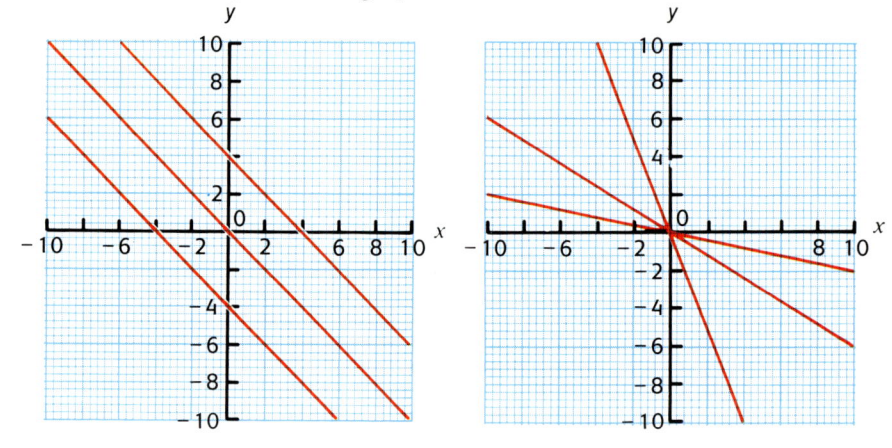

... Exploring graphs

Graph matching

1. Match the graph to the equation.

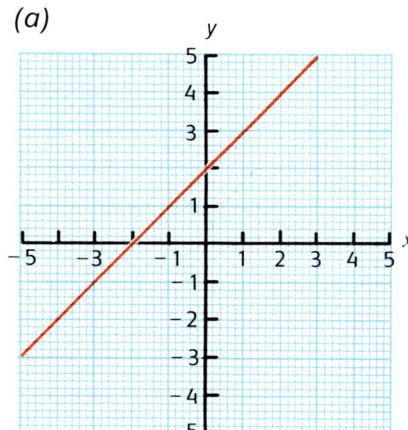

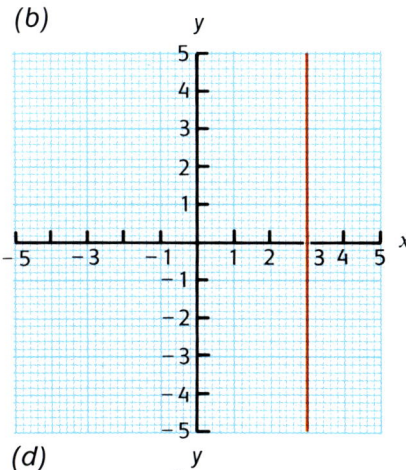

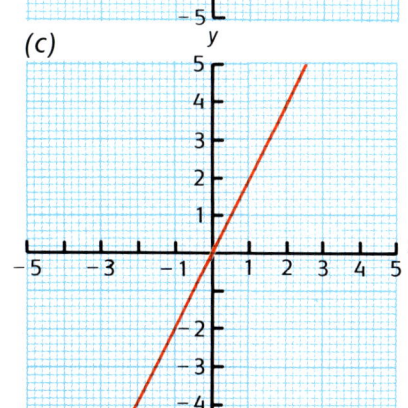

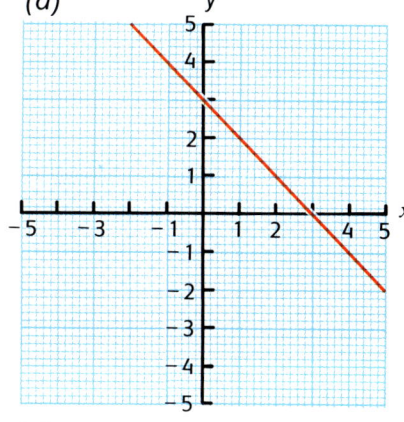

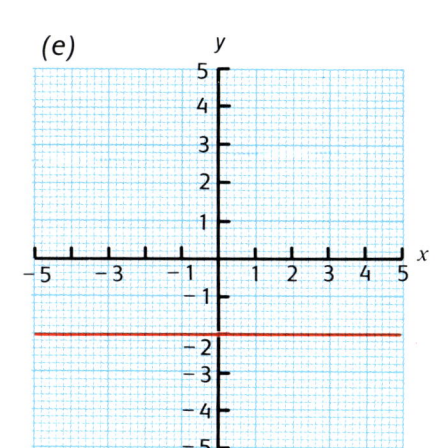

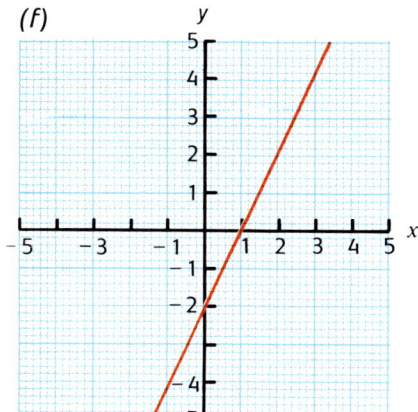

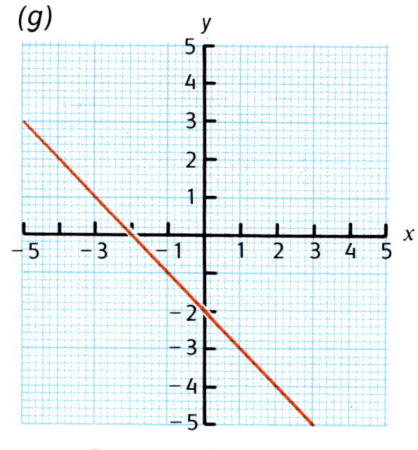

(a) (b) (c) (d) (e) (f) (g)

$y = 3 - x$ $y = 2x$ $x = 3$ $y = x + 2$ $y = -2$ $y = 2x - 2$

2. What is the equation of the remaining graph?

Y 9 ALGEBRA – C

Unit 8 Spreadsheets and sequences

Spreadsheet sequences

A calculator is useful for doing the arithmetic for sequences but it only gives one number at a time. A computer spreadsheet will do the arithmetic and will also make a string of numbers.

Suppose you want to make the sequence 10, 20, 30, 40 . . .

- Put 10 in the first cell (data or numbers).
- Put the rule `cell 1 + 10` in the next cell down (formula).

  20 appears in this cell.

- Copy the formula down the column as far as you want.

  30, 40, 50 . . . appear in the cells.

- Try this example for yourself on a spreadsheet.

  When you think you know how the spreadsheet works, try to make these sequences.

  1. Write down the tenth term for each:

     1 2 3 4 5 . . .

     2 4 6 8 . . .

     1 3 5 7 9 . . .

     5 10 15 20 . . .

     7 14 21 28 . . .

     1 2 4 8 16 . . .

     1 4 9 16 25 . . .

     1 2 3 5 8 13 . . .

  For the last two the formula is rather different.

  If you want help see the ideas on page 55.

LN S2, S3

... Spreadsheets and sequences

... using two columns

You have met this sequence a number of times –

1   3   6   10   15   21 . . .

1. Write down how it continues.
2. What is this sequence called?

■ To make this sequence on a spreadsheet you will need two columns:

	Column A	Column B
row 1	1	1
row 2	2	3
row 3	3	6
row 4	4	10
row 5	5	15

This shows me A4 + B3 gives B4

Your formula will be something like B2 = A2 + B1 (depending on your particular spreadsheet version)

■ Produce the triangle numbers on your spreadsheet and save.

☐ Use it to check your answers to 'Curve stitching' on page 34.

In this example the relationship is simpler:

1   2
2   4
3   6
4   8   → B4 = 2 × A4
5   10

■ Produce even numbers on your spreadsheet and save.

■ Now do the same with:
 – square numbers
 – odd numbers.

LN S2, S3

Y 9 ALGEBRA – C

... Spreadsheets and sequences

S LN S2, S3

Guessing formulae

Kelly, Scott and Jerry played a computer spreadsheet game.

Kelly set up a formula.

The other two suggested input numbers and watched the output after the numbers had been typed in.

The aim of the game is to guess the formula correctly.

■ Now it's your turn!

It will take three players to play the game.

You are allowed as many input numbers and as much discussion as you want but you only have one guess at the formula.

Here is the screen after five inputs:

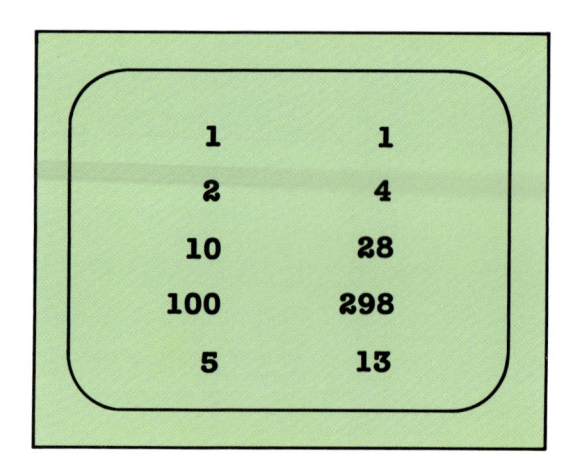

1	1
2	4
10	28
100	298
5	13

■ Can you guess the formula?

☐ Play the game taking it in turns to choose the formula.

Beware! Formulae can get very complicated so it is a good idea to make limits — for example, no numbers greater than five.

... Spreadsheets and sequences

Well matched

dead matches

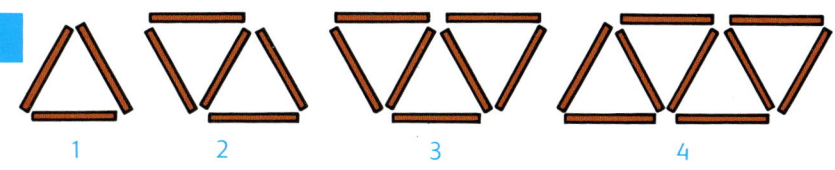

LN S2, S3

1 2 3 4

- Use matches to build these patterns of triangles.
- Put your results on a spreadsheet or in a table.

Triangles (A)	Matches (B)
1	3
2	5
3	7
4	9

- Can you see a link between the number of triangles and number of matches?
1. Work out a formula for this link.
- Check your prediction by putting your formula into the spreadsheet on a new line underneath the table.
- Do you get the same numbers as column *B*?
2. How many matches would you need for 100 triangles?
- Now look at this pattern of squares built from matches.

3. Try to work out a formula for this sequence.
4. How many do you need for 100 squares?
- Make up a sequence of your own.

Y 9 ALGEBRA – C

... Spreadsheets and sequences

Farmer's fences

A farmer has 30 m of fencing to make a sheep pen.

1. What is the area of this sheep pen measuring 9 m by 6 m?

   What is the greatest area she can enclose using her 30 m of fencing?

   First, cut a strip of paper 30 cm long and about 2 cm wide to act as your fence.

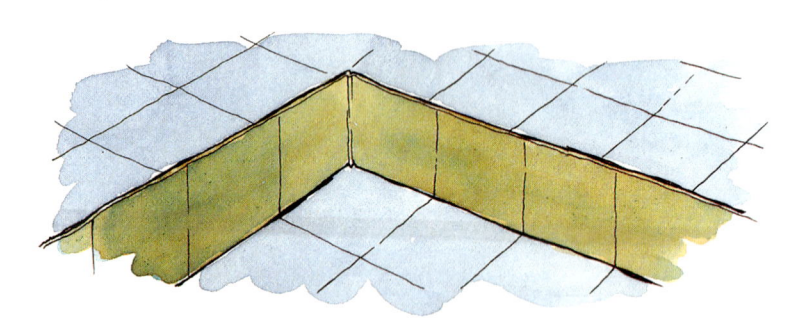

LN S2, S3

Then use a spreadsheet to make a table like this.

Length (A)	Width (B)	Total length (C)	Area (D)
9	6	30	?

2. Use a formula for area to complete the spreadsheet column D.

3. Can you see where else to use a formula?

   The farmer has an idea.

   She can use a hedge for one side of the sheep pen.

   Work out the different areas she can make now.

   What is the largest area she can enclose?

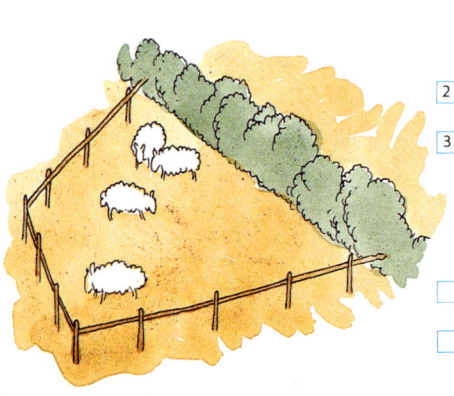

Unit 9 Making and solving equations

- Cut out the cards and on the back of the *x* cards write the numbers from one to fifteen.
- Make up a number sentence.

  I'll do 4 + 6 = 10.

- Turn over one of the number cards.

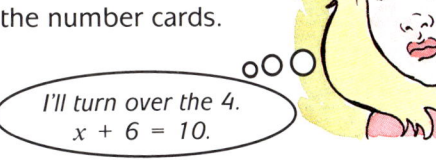

  I'll turn over the 4.
  x + 6 = 10.

- Swap your sentence with another person.
- For the sentence you have been given, work out what number is under the *x*.
- ☐ Do this a few times.
- ☐ Try sentences like 6 = 10 − 4 and 2 × 8 = 16

Does it make any difference which number in the sentence you turn over?

Does it make it easier or harder to solve the equation?

1. Try to solve these and find the value of *x*

   $x + 1 = 7$ $3x = 15$ $x \div 4 = 12$ $2x + 4 = 8$

- Make up some more equations for your group to solve.

  Agree some rules so that the equations are not too difficult to solve, for example, only numbers less than ten.

  The answer is five.

- ☐ How many equations can you find where the solution is five?
- ☐ Make a group display of all the equations you can find with an answer five.

Y 9 ALGEBRA − C

... Making and solving equations

Flags

✓ 📄 5

The [× 2] flag turns these inputs into outputs.

input		output
2	→	4
3	→	6
6	→	12
4	→	8

[1] What operation reverses this? So that:

4	→	2
6	→	3
12	→	6
8	→	4

☐ Write you answer on the back of the [× 2] flag.

■ Find the inverses for each of the other flags.

For a reminder about inverses, turn to page 23.

☐ Write them on the back of each one.

■ Choose a flag and a number as an input.

■ Calculate the input.

■ Write a sentence like this: 5   [+ 6]   11

■ Turn the flag over.

For example this might give: 5   [− 6]   11

■ Read this from right to left on the direction of the flag.

Eleven minus six gives five.

■ With your partner, make some more sentences like this.

Turn the flag over.

Is the statement true this way round?

Now choose a flag and an output, like this: ?   [× 2]   16

■ Turn the flag over. Find the unknown input.

■ Make up some more puzzles like this.

Give them to your partner to solve and find the input.

... Making and solving equations

Two flags

✓ 5 with inverses written on the back of each flag

■ Choose an input and use two flags to complete a sentence, like this:

4 ▸ × 2 ▸ − 1 ▸ 7.

■ Turn the flags over.

■ Read from right to left following the direction of the flags.

[1] Is the sentence still true?

■ Try this a few times. Check that the sentence is still true when you turn over the flags.

■ Now make up a sentence using two flags and an output.

For example:

? ▸ + 6 ▸ × 2 ▸ 22

■ Turn the flags over. Calculate the input.

■ Turn the flags over again. Check that the sentence is true.

☐ Try this a few times.

[2] Find the inputs in these examples:

? ▸ + 1 ▸ × 3 ▸ 18

? ▸ − 1 ▸ × 3 ▸ 18

? ▸ × 2 ▸ + 5 ▸ 17

? ▸ + 5 ▸ × 2 ▸ 18

■ Make up some more examples like this.

Give them to your partner to solve.

■ Investigate using three flags with your partner.

Let's try using three flags.

Will it still work?

Y 9 ALGEBRA − C

... Making and solving equations

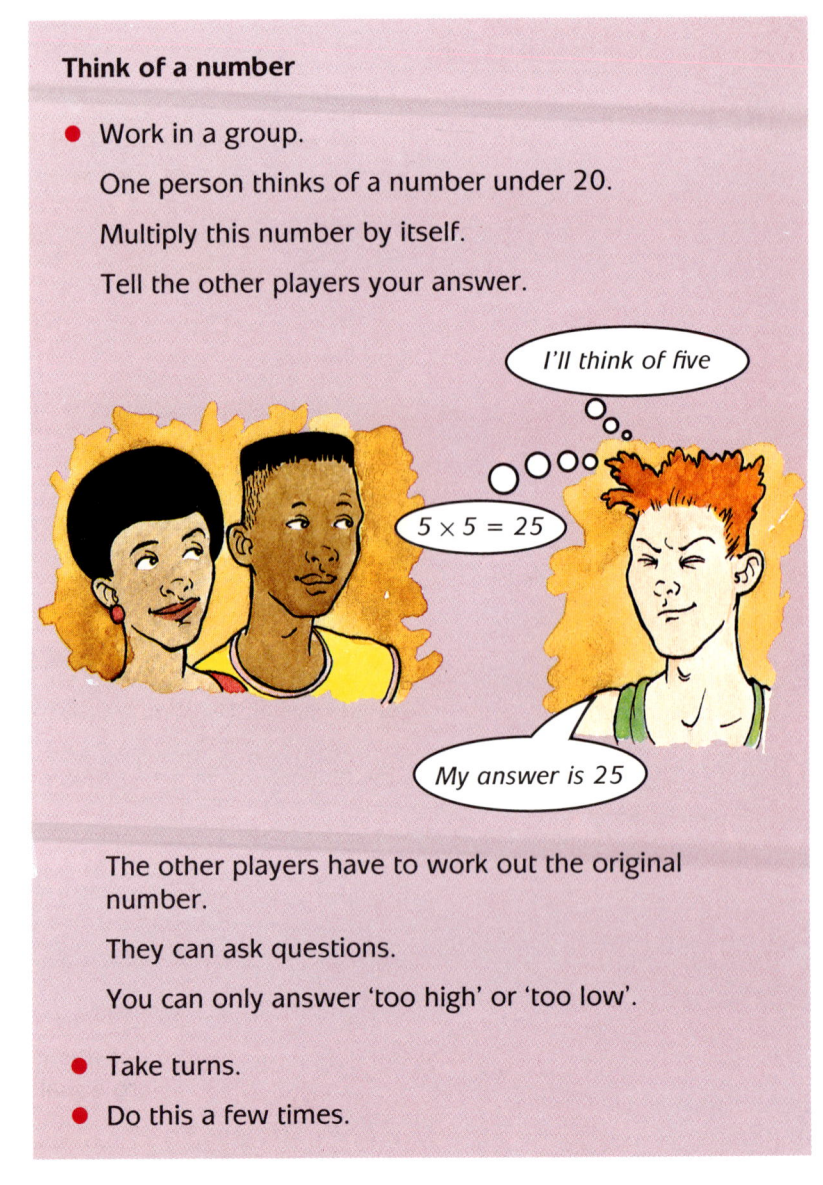

Think of a number

- Work in a group.

  One person thinks of a number under 20.

  Multiply this number by itself.

  Tell the other players your answer.

  I'll think of five

  $5 \times 5 = 25$

  My answer is 25

  The other players have to work out the original number.

  They can ask questions.

  You can only answer 'too high' or 'too low'.

- Take turns.
- Do this a few times.

■ What is the smallest number of guesses needed to find the original number?

■ Investigate what happens when you start with a decimal number.

■ Investigate what happens when you start with a negative number.

... Making and solving equations

Trial and improvement

This is a useful method for solving equations.

Suppose your group has to solve $x^2 = 15$

$3 \times 3 = 9$ so x is greater than 3.

$4 \times 4 = 16$ so x is in between 3 and 4.

- Keep a record like this:

x	x^2	
3	9	too small
4	16	too big
3.5	...	.....
...		
...		

- Keep trying different values of x so that you get closer and closer to 15. How many tries did it take?

- Try to solve $x^2 = 17$ in fewer tries.

- How can you adapt your method to solve $x^2 + 3 = 14$?

- Try a table like this:

x	x^2	$x^2 + 3$	
3	9	12	too small
4	16	17	too big
...	...	→	get this number to equal 14

Using trial and improvement on a graphic calculator, your screen might look like the one on the left.

Using ▲ will allow you to edit each line.

The calculator evaluates $x^2 + 3$, with $x = 3$.

```
3² + 3
            12
4² + 3
            19
```

- You have to get this equal to 14

- In your group, make up some more equations to solve using this method.

Y 9 ALGEBRA – C

... Making and solving equations

Solving by graphs

G8C, 8T

This is the graph of $y = 3x + 1$. It shows that when $y = 10$, $x = 3$.

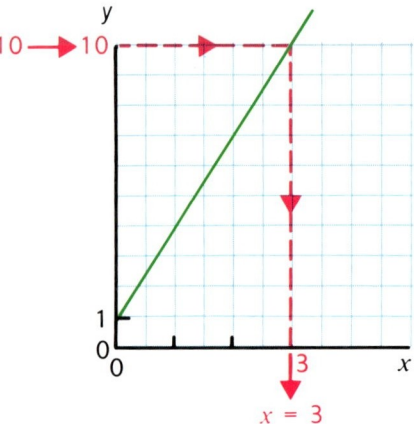

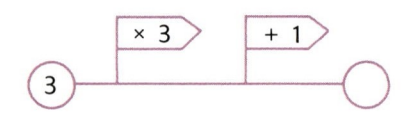

$x = 3$ is the solution of $3x + 1 = 10$

- Check this using this flag diagram

□ Draw the graph of $y = 3x + 1$.

[1] Use your graph to find the solutions of:

(a) $3x + 1 = 7$

(b) $3x + 1 = 5$.

- Check your solutions using flag diagrams.

G8C, 8T

□ Draw the graph of $y = 2x - 1$

LN P3

[2] Use your graph to solve:

(a) $2x - 1 = 11$

(b) $2x - 1 = 6$.

- Check your solutions each time.

[3] By drawing a suitable graph, solve:

(a) $10 - 2x = 5$

(b) $10 - 2x = 14$.

- Check your solutions.

□ Solve the equations in question 1, page 59 by drawing suitable graphs.